Hou

"Susan's on a roll again! More wise and witty insights to laugh us down the highway."

—Willie Nelson, singer, songwriter, actor, and author

"Susan Goldfein has done it again with this new volume of human truths and frailties. She never ceases to be hilarious as she illuminates our everyday tendencies. She is our mirror on the wall."

—Julie Gilbert, novelist, biographer, playwright, and teacher

"Fasten your seat belts, don a pair of fun sunnies, and put the top down—Susan is about to take you on a joyride through the golden years. Fully packed with wry wit and wisdom, this book will have you laughing and nodding the whole way."

—Terri Bryce Reeves, editor, *Lifestyles After 50*

"Take a gallon of creativity. Mix with a pint of snarky humor, a cup of insight, a dollop of spice, and sprinkle with laughter. What you've got is Susan Goldfein at her best. Susan takes ordinary living to an art form. She makes everyday experiences a formidable challenge, as she gracefully guides us through 'age-hood' with her unique style and wit, making every senior moment a recipe to treasure."

—Judith Marks-White, author of *Seducing Harry*
and *Bachelor Degree*

HOW TO COMPLAIN

when there's nothing to complain about

Susan Goldfein

HOW TO COMPLAIN

when there's nothing to complain about

more thoughts about life
from the far side of the hill

SUSAN GOLDFEIN

The essays in this collection have previously appeared on the author's blog www.SusansUnfilteredWit.com.

Illustrations by Kristine Lucco
Cover Illustration by John T. Takai
Author Photo by Mel Abfier

Library of Congress Cataloging-in-Publication Data

Goldfein, Susan
How to Complain When There's Nothing to Complain About:
More Thoughts About Life from the Far Side of the Hill

p. cm.

Paperback ISBN: 978-1-947708-23-5

Ebook ISBN: 978-1-947708-24-2

Library of Congress Control Number: 2018952693

10 9 8 7 6 5 4 3 2 1

First Edition, December 2018

 CITRINE PUBLISHING
Asheville, North Carolina, U.S.A.
(828) 585 - 7030
Publisher@CitrinePublishing.com
www.CitrinePublishing.com

FOR LARRY,
AGAIN AND ALWAYS

CONTENTS

HOW DID I GET HERE?

HOW TO COMPLAIN...

Contents

ENDING ON A HIGH NOTE

Introduction

I decided to publish a second book because, in the long run, doing so was cheaper than therapy, and a lot less risky than murder.

Humor continues to be my weapon of choice to combat the foibles of domestic life, the indignities of aging in an ageist society, ridiculous social trends, and whatever piece of nuttiness I happen to be observing that day. So instead of lying on a couch, or picking up a sharp instrument, I write.

Someone once said, and I wish it had been my own clever comment, "When life throws you punches, make punchlines." This works for me.

Further encouragement to produce a second volume of essays came from the fact that my first book actually won three awards. Not bad for an author of personal essays who was neither a Hollywood celebrity or someone who had an affair with a current or former President of the United States.

And, if you permit me to expand on my bragging rights, (What choice do you have?) as of September 2017, I have been engaged to write a humor column for a monthly publication entitled *Lifestyles After 50*. This is an especially good fit for me since my current age renders me highly qualified to discuss life after fifty. And I'm not at all lamenting this fact. Despite all claims from cosmetic companies, there is really only one thing that can actually halt the aging process. And I strongly favor the alternative of celebrating additional birthdays.

As with my first book, *How Old Am I in Dog Years?,* my material comes from life. While almost nothing is off-limits,

I do tend to steer clear of politics, religion, and my family, with one exception: my husband is not exempt. After all, what humor writer worth her keyboard would bypass marriage as a bottomless source of fodder? And I love him all the more for being such a good sport.

These otherwise random essays have been shuffled and placed under five different topic headings ranging from "Spousal Privilege" to the depths of "How to Complain," but always "Ending on a High Note." I've selected the essays I've found the most personally therapeutic. Hopefully, they'll succeed in reducing your couch time as well.

Susan Goldfein
Palm Beach, Florida
October 2018

SPOUSAL PRIVILEGE

As Long as You're Up...

At times I feel like I've been transported back to the sixties and am trapped in that old ad for Grant's Scotch. Remember that ad? Don't try to tell me you weren't born yet. (Well, some of you weren't born yet, but very few.)

I'm not sure how many bottles of whiskey they sold, but the slogan, "As long as you're up, get me a Grant's," had a major impact on popular culture. It went viral before there was such a thing as "viral." It was a subject of a famous *New Yorker* cartoon and found a home in the *Yale Book of Quotations* in the company of such other blockbusters as, "I can't believe I ate the whole thing."

The Grant's ads were staged to ooze upper-class sophistication. Each one featured a photograph of an affluent-looking, elegant, well-dressed, not-so-young man or woman. The ultra-thin, perfectly coiffed, attractive woman was dressed in a simple, but clearly expensive gown, and was sitting in a chair which looked like it was recently bought at auction from Sotheby's.

The handsome, graying-at-the-temples-with-just-the-right-amount-of-gray man was in a tuxedo, also sitting. Each body was turned slightly as if addressing an invisible off-stage partner.

Although the ad for Grant's Scotch faded from usage a long time ago, I'm happy to say that the slogan, at least the first half of it, is alive and well and living in our house. With some slight revisions.

The man (my husband) is not wearing a tuxedo, but is instead dressed in golf shorts. His graying temples can no longer be distinguished from the rest of his hair color, and the chair he sits in was purchased for comfort rather than its antique value.

The woman (me) does not wear a gown, but is attired in jeans and a T-shirt, and is not now, and never has been, as thin as the woman in the ad.

However, the operative words remain unchanged: "As long as you're up…"

Perhaps in every long-term relationship there emerges a "requestor" and a "requestee." These roles are not so easily predictable, because in my experience, they're not always gender-dependent. Not counting extenuating circumstances, like a broken leg, for instance, women are just as capable as men when it comes to asking for little favors, and men can be just as compliant as women in granting them.

In my relationship, however, I have become the "requestee." Possibly it's my inability to sit in one place for extended periods of time that has cast me in this role. So, as I am frequently up and about during the course of an hour-long TV show, it does not seem unreasonable that a voice from the other room calls out, "As long as you're up, get me a

4

glass of club soda." Although he swears he has no recollection of ever seeing that ad, the words seemed to flow from him as easily as scotch over ice.

It's not always club soda. Sometimes it's a piece of chocolate. Or it could be ice cream. Or a sweater because he's chilly. Really, it's all okay. I'm happy to do it. As long as I'm up.

Occasionally, however, a request with a slightly different tone of voice finds its way into our marital discourse. This request is preceded by, "If you're getting up…," or, "When you go upstairs…," and usually occurs when I've been in a holding pattern in my chair for longer than usual. These, of course, are not-so-subtle indications that my darling is desirous of something, and would prefer not to get it for himself. This causes me to look at him through narrowed eyes, but more often than not, I will grant him his favor.

Have my hyperactive tendencies created a monster, or at the very least, a spoiled spouse? Not really. Because at the end of the day, I know there is a balance. I bring him a pillow, and he brings me a…remind me, what is it that he brings me?

Oh yes, the favors do go both ways. He graciously plays golf with me on Sundays, which cannot be much fun for him, and he doesn't make me watch football, which would never be any fun for me.

Most importantly, he is someone that I can rely on, someone who is always there for me, someone who loves me unconditionally. So I will happily continue to bestow him favors. As long as I'm up!

State of the Reunion

I am frequently confronted by an occurrence that appears to be a statistical improbability but is nevertheless true.

My husband and I are out for the evening. Our destination is of little importance. We could be in line to purchase movie tickets, or waiting for our table in a restaurant. Or even preparing to board the first flight to Mars. It doesn't matter. Invariably he will run into a guy he knows from high school.

What makes this so astonishing is that his high school class had all of 200 students, while my class had about 900. And yet, I bump into nobody.

So these old acquaintances (frequently, the wife is a hometown girl as well) acknowledge each other with great surprise and delight, and sit down and join us at the dinner table. Or plan to meet up after the movie for coffee. What ensues for them is a thoroughly enjoyable three-way conversation about old times. I just sit there and smile.

My husband grew up in a small town on Long Island, New York. For those of you not from the New York area, Long

Island is a strip of land that is actually a part of Brooklyn, although its inhabitants would rather jump in the Long Island Sound with rocks in their pockets than admit to that.

In addition to being given fluorinated water to prevent cavities, and inoculations against whooping cough, I am firmly convinced that children growing up in or near his town in the above-mentioned location, were implanted with a homing device that enables them to find each other in whatever hemisphere they happen to be residing. Or vacationing in. Or golfing in. Or visiting the proctologist in. I refuse to believe that these encounters are mere coincidence.

As a result, I have become a silent participant in a fairly steady stream of both informal and formal get-togethers during which I witness, somewhat enviously, their nostalgia.

Just this winter alone, there have been three such occasions, and as an observer, I have begun to notice a pattern. Besides the goodwill, the pleasure of seeing one another, and some requisite whining about how their golf games are deteriorating, each reunion seems to have three essential ingredients. These are: "The Medical Update," "The Geography Game," and an activity that I have named, "Alive or Dead?"

The Medical Update consists of a general review of everyone's body parts. In this segment we are informed about recent hip surgeries, knee replacements, shoulder operations, and about who knows the absolute best doctor to see if you need work on your right arm between the elbow and the wrist. This inventory may or may not be followed up with what has come to be known as the "organ recital," and includes any pertinent information about livers, kidneys, pancreases, and of course, hearts. Cholesterol count is optional.

The Geography Game is one of my personal favorites, although it can become a little contentious. This is the part of the evening when those who are no longer living in the home town ask those who are about historic landmarks.

"Remember Romeo's Pizza Parlor on Main Street? Is it still there?"

"That wasn't on Main Street. That was on Jones Street, across from the movies."

"No it wasn't; you're thinking of the ice cream parlor."

"You think I don't know the difference between an ice cream parlor and a pizza parlor?"

Similar inquiries take place regarding the bowling alley, kosher butcher, and the pharmacy where you could get the best egg creams. Or was that malteds?

Finally, we arrive at that inevitable part of the evening when the discussion turns to those former classmates who are not present at the current gathering.

"Whatever happened to Bill Mason?"

"Didn't he die recently?"

"Are you crazy? He isn't dead. I just spoke to him at a member-guest."

"Are you sure you spoke to him? Because I heard he was dead."

At a typical reunion, at least five other people are discussed in this manner before dessert is served.

Despite the small disagreements about what was where, and if so-and-so is "Alive or Dead?," the evening is congenial, and thoroughly enjoyed by everyone. Even me, although I'm not an integral part of the original group.

And I'm sure it would be not one iota different if it were my old neighborhood and my high school friends being discussed. If only I could find them.

People of Brooklyn, you have got to get out more!

DIY?

I am of the firm opinion that if a project is advertised as something you can do yourself, it should be exactly that. Yourself. Alone. No assistance required. And therefore, no possibility of discord with The Significant Other.

It is with this belief that, singularly, I have tackled furniture purchases from Ikea and Crate and Barrel, spending many satisfying moments on the floor with my Phillips-head screw driver, fitting Part A into Part B, and praying that this time, they have included the proper-sized screws in the little plastic bag with the assortment of fasteners.

When I'm finally finished, certain that I have successfully included all of the provided pieces, and have located my right leg, which has fallen asleep during the process, I stand proudly in front of my newly assembled bookcase. Yay me!

So it was without trepidation, and with the utmost confidence, that I listened to my husband inform me that on the Internet he had found the perfect teak bench to grace our newly landscaped backyard, upon which we would happily sit for hours, enjoying the water view. It was good-looking, well-priced, and, what did it say in the fine print? Assembly required? No problem for the Ikea Queen.

"Yes," I encouraged, "by all means, order it." So he did.

Five days later, a large truck pulled up to our house and unloaded a massive package that had to be way more than bench parts. "Hold on," I told the driver. "I don't remember ordering a refrigerator." He checked his clipboard, and assured me that this was definitely my delivery.

I allowed him to wheel the monster to my backyard, signed the delivery slip, and helplessly watched him leave. Had he just wished me good luck?

I forlornly stood there, staring at this huge thing wrapped in ominous-looking black plastic. This was no slim and friendly Ikea box. Instead, it looked like a bag of refuse from a dinner party hosted by the Jolly Green Giant!

I managed to get close enough to tear off the envelope containing the packing slip and the assembly instructions. I started feeling somewhat better as I began to read the directions. That is, until I came to the part that said, "Have someone hold Part B while you attach Part C."

Now real fear had struck. Husband-and-wife teams could be a little risky. I'd heard of divorce as an outcome of couples playing bridge or tennis together. And who really knew what went on behind the scenes between Lucy and Desi, Stiller and Meara, Burns and Allen?

In our particular case, I have considered murder more than once as my husband and I have endeavored to cooperate on accomplishing domestic tasks. Take, for example, the time we had to install the removable pool barrier before our grandchildren's visit. We began as consenting adults, then quickly decomposed.

"You're starting in the wrong place."

"Who says?"

"You're supposed to start here, not there."

"Where is it written?"

"You're unrolling it backwards."

"No, I'm not, you are."

"Stop pulling so hard."

"I'm not pulling."

"Yes, you are!"

Last time I heard dialogue like this was when I took my children to the playground. Or was it last spring when we decided to clean out the garage? I would have considered death by drowning, but my husband happens to be a good swimmer.

So, it was with considerable caution that I began to rip away at the enormous black garbage bag, the cardboard, and finally the inner plastic wrapping, to reveal the parts innocently awaiting assemblage to become our new bench.

I was ready to face the potential of adversity. I reasoned that after this was over, even if we don't talk for the next two days, I would have fodder for a new essay.

"Okay," I timidly called out, "let's do it."

With each step representing a new possibility for conflict and blame, my mental notepad was ready and the pencil poised.

What a disappointment! The process went exceedingly well. Hard to believe, but there were no accusations, not even when we put the legs on backwards and had to start over. And where did that thin slat of wood belong? It wasn't on the instruction sheet. But together, we calmly figured it out.

Who were these two people who had worked together so well? Do I know them? Have we reached a kinder, gentler level in our relationship, or am I reading too much into this success?

Stay tuned. I'll let you know how it goes the next time we have to reinstall the pool barrier.

Parting is Such Sweet Sorrow

When it comes to decluttering, the world seems to consist of two types of people: those who are able to divest themselves of inanimate objects once they've outlived their usefulness, and those who would sentimentally cling to an old rubber band.

Darned if I know why letting go of things is so difficult for some people, and so much easier for others, but I do know this: if you happen to be living with someone who is a "keeper" and you are inclined the other way, I suggest purchasing a helmet in preparation for repeatedly running up against that stone wall. Trust me. I speak from experience.

I should have recognized my husband's discarding disorder back when we were dating, and he proudly pointed out how he had deconstructed and reconstructed a very large piece of furniture to occupy a small corner of his small living room. "That must have been costly," I offered as I gazed at the not-very-attractive results. "Wouldn't you have been better off getting something new that would fit?"

"And throw away that perfectly good breakfront?" he replied incredulously. "Besides, it used to belong to my ex-mother-in-law."

I must have been blinded by love. I missed that red flag completely.

Throughout our years together, we have continued to engage in these little skirmishes regarding possessions. Among the notable incidents was the clash over the cardigan sweater, the color of which is reminiscent of a jar of French's mustard long past the "use by" date. There are small holes in the right sleeve, and a couple of stains on the front that have baffled the dry cleaning experts. I lost that conflict.

I also lost the battle over the forty-year-old pair of shoes, the old lamp with the crooked shade, and the outdated set of law books that probably haven't been relevant since the turn of the century. Not this century, the last one.

For a while there had been an uneasy peace in our war over useless objects. That is, until the other day.

Staring at the collection of loose papers and file folders that were threatening to completely occupy the living room, we agreed that the time had come for my husband to have a desk, and to return the sofa to its intended purpose.

After considerable analysis of our floor plan, we realized that the only way to properly accommodate a desk was to divest ourselves of an existing piece of furniture that might be called a buffet, or a server, or a credenza; I've never really been sure of the difference. Whatever the proper name, it had long ceased to have any practical function, and had become a dumping place for other unnecessary articles that I had failed to throw away when my husband's back was turned.

"Great," I said. "It's about time. It was starting to become a bit of an eyesore."

"But we've had it for such a long time. We can't get rid of it just like that," he said with an unsuccessful attempt at snapping his fingers.

Even without the accompanying finger snap, I knew where this was heading. So I went to look for the helmet.

"All the more reason to let it go," I said in my best practical voice.

"But we bought it for our very first apartment. Don't you remember? I can still picture the shop. It was that antique store on 10th Avenue. It was a Sunday. It was 4:00 PM, and it was raining."

"What color were the salesman's eyes?" I retorted, trying, but failing to hide the sarcasm. I also reminded him that the term "antique" store was a liberal application of that label. He ignored me and went on, "Isn't there somewhere else we can use it? What if we cut off the legs and...?"

"No," I said abruptly. "No carpentry." I had better nip this in the bud. "We have to let it go."

"Maybe there's someone in the family who would want it. Then we could at least ask for visitation rights." I thought about this for five seconds, maybe four.

"Can't think of anyone," I replied.

"How about Aunt Sally?" he queried.

"She might have liked it," I agreed, "but she died six months ago."

"Oh, right."

So for the next half-hour we worked our way through the entire roster of immediate family members, first cousins, and second cousins once removed. After I got him to agree it was impractical to even think about shipping a large piece of furniture to Uncle Sid's ex-wife in Alaska, he finally capitulated. Was victory actually mine?

Removing the helmet, I rushed to the phone to call Goodwill. I knew full well it was only a matter of time before he figured out how to turn the darn thing into a planter.

Becoming the Quibblers

When I was a young married person, I would sometimes find myself in the company of an older married couple who had been together for a very long time. And it was impossible not to notice that they would frequently disagree over the most unimportant subjects. And this disagreement would invariably lead to an argument.

I used to wonder to myself if this was the way they had been communicating for the past forty years, and if so, they had done a very good job of concealing their battle scars. Or, could the pattern of their discourse be something more recent? And if so, which wedding anniversary was the one that became the fatal turning point?

The image of the quarreling older couple became front and center in my mind as my husband and I celebrated another year of marriage. And I feared that we might have reached that critical year.

I say this now, because the other day, as we were "discussing" the best way to slice a bagel, (I was slicing, he was fault-finding) we were definitely on the brink of becoming The Quibblers.

So what exactly is quibbling? While the word may sound like a British board game, it is, in reality, a verbal exchange that involves arguing about something that really doesn't matter.

Had this been the only incident, it would have gone unnoticed. He's entitled to his views about bagel-cutting. But since he's never had to rush me to the ER with a sliced palm, he could just look away and keep his opinions to himself. And if I do slice my palm, it will be all his fault, so he should stop reminding me to be careful.

But that was *not* the only incident. A pattern was definitely emerging. The recent delivery from Amazon Prime had evolved into a five-minute quibble about the best way to open the box, which obviously had been sealed by some very unhappy or highly sadistic warehouse worker.

The proper place to store the butter in the refrigerator so it would not be hidden by larger objects became another issue for trivial pursuit. (So, big deal. Sometimes you have to move the milk container to find the butter.)

What really is the correct way to hang the dog's leash? Because if you do it this way instead of that way, it keeps falling off the hook!

Or, how do we get from here to there, when both ways are equally as good?

And where is the best place to leave messages so that the person who is most oblivious (him) would not fail to see them?

I could go on with more examples, but I'm sure by now you know what I mean. Whatever happened to arguing about really important things, like the true position of the toilet seat?

I don't believe that quibbling is limited to married couples. It can exist between siblings or good friends. Any close relationship is at risk. Ever witness two women in a kitchen trying to put a meal together? They're likely to disagree over the best way to boil water.

So how did we arrive at this petty place? Perhaps it's the result of too much togetherness. Or just being older and more set in our ways, convinced that each of us knows best. I do, of course.

I wonder if quibbling is inevitable in a long-term relationship? Perhaps so, but at the same time, it can remain quite benign if we can step back and laugh at ourselves.

But there is a slippery slope. The Quibble, left unchecked, has the potential to degrade into The Bicker.

The Bicker is quibbling with an edge. Whereas quibbling is relatively mild-mannered, bickering can be petulant and bad-tempered…like in that old radio show, where Blanche (Frances Langford) would awaken John (Don Ameche) in the middle of the night so she could argue with him. (Of course, I was just a child at the time, but I remember my parents listening to it.)

So, my dear, as an anniversary gift to each other, let's not let the quibbling run amok. Because "Becoming the Bickersons" is an essay I never want to write.

You Gotta Love Him!

So I'm sitting at my desk trying to write this essay. Instead, I'm allowing my mind to wander and my attention to be distracted. My eyes should be focused on the screen while my fingers fly over the keyboard. But every few minutes I swivel my chair to the right and stare at what may turn out to be one of the worst decisions we've ever made, or our personal Fountain of Youth.

We have a new dog!

I know there are those of you who will immediately conclude that we have finally lost what remained of our marbles. But you pet lovers will be supportive. Won't you?

This action was not part of our long-range plan. We are capable of rational thought. Having recently lost our second dog, we had decided it would be sensible to wait awhile, to exist in a state of doglessness and see how we felt.

But I caved to an impulse. You'd think I'd learn. Last time I succumbed to an impulse I dyed my hair purple, a decision which left me completely miserable, as the color coordinated with nothing in my wardrobe.

(Pause. I'm going to pet the dog now.)

If there is blame to be laid, then it must certainly land on my dear spouse. He never should have left me alone last Saturday when I was feeling particularly sad and depressed over the loss of our beloved Davis, the Lab. Of course, I never told him I was feeling particularly sad and depressed as I watched him go off to his golf game. But after all these years of marriage, is it too much to expect that he just *know?*

After he left, I thought about going shopping to cope with my grief. My favorite boutique was having a designer trunk show, something that normally would arouse my endorphins. But I couldn't muster enthusiasm, which really caused me a good deal of concern. When a woman can't get energized by the prospect of a shopping trip, you know she's ready for the latest psychotropic cocktail.

(Pause. I'm going to play with the dog now.)

I'm back. Where was I? Oh, yes, psychotropics. But not being a big fan of drugs, I did the only other thing that would ease my pain. I contacted The Dog Lady.

The Dog Lady's name, phone number, and email address was sitting in a folder for such time, if ever, that we would be ready for our next pooch.

We, that is, myself and He Who Can't Read Minds, had already discussed the type of dog we would get *if* we were ever to get another dog. And this particular Dog Lady was our source.

I told myself it was a harmless email, merely exploratory. Probably there would be no dogs to our liking for a long, long time. Probably our names had to be placed on a waiting list. Probably she would immediately determine we were too old to be doing this. Probably all of the above would be true, so it was perfectly safe to send the email.

(Pause. He's looking at me. I need to hold him.)

Probably, I was wrong. No, *definitely* I was wrong. Dog Lady responded within ten minutes, stating that, after reading my requirements, she just happened to have the perfect dog for us. Perhaps if she hadn't sent the photo, I could have let it go. As I went twirling around the house, it was clear that my spirits had lifted.

When he finally arrived home, I shared the photo with He Who Can't Read Minds, and it was quite something to see a grown man melt!

We met Sam on a Tuesday. He was an eleven-month-old Jack Russell, who liked to be held and drenched us with kisses. He was every bit as cute as his picture, with personality to match, and we were smitten.

Once we made the commitment, I had to prepare for Sam's arrival, which meant buying what was necessary to keep him, and our home, safe. Although he was almost a year old, it would be awhile before he outgrew his puppyish ways. After my fourth trip to the store, I realized I should have thrown myself a puppy shower, and registered at Petco.

(Pause. Sam needs more water.)

We have now had Sam with us for a grand total of four days, and we have become fast friends. He truly is the dog of our dreams, had we been dreaming about a dog.

We look at each other, that is, He Who Can't and me, and wonder what we've done, as Sam bounds back and forth from one to the other. But the truth is we haven't stopped smiling.

Perhaps Sam will wear us out. Or perhaps he will keep us young. My money is on the latter.

And, yes, there is a chance that Sam will outlive us. In which case, we are considering adding a codicil to our will. Our kids will have to deal with sharing our assets six ways, instead of five. Just look at that face. Tell me, wouldn't you immediately call your lawyer?

(Okay, Sam. I'm all yours now.)

If I Should Die Before You...

Garbage bags
This way

Please don't stop reading. I promise that, despite the title, what follows is not a downer. Rather, it's an observation, a practical consideration, and maybe even a little bit funny.

What precipitated my seemingly somber reflection was an actual conversation I had with my husband, a semi-retired attorney, who, for the past three years, has been vowing that this year would be the last. However, you did notice that the prefix is still attached to the verb?

But before I relate the conversation, let me set the scene. One recent morning, I took a risk and stepped into his home office. "Why a risk?" you might ask. Because, upon crossing the threshold there is imminent danger of tripping over stacks of file folders piled on the floor, slipping on fallen pens, and experiencing vertigo as you observe the chaos surrounding his person as he sits on the small loveseat, diligently engrossed. He is unaware that our little dog, Sam, has been busy removing crumpled papers from his overflowing waste basket and turning them into confetti.

I, of course, notice this immediately, as I silently strategize about the best way to maneuver the vacuum cleaner so as not to disturb the piles. Forgetting why I put my life on the line in the first place, my focus is now on the waste basket. And so the dialogue begins:

"Ahem, honey…?" He looks up. "I can't help but notice that the waste basket is brimming over, and the dog is engaged in an arts and crafts project."

"Oh, right," he says. "If you would get me a garbage bag, I'll empty it right now."

Get him a garbage bag? My feminist dander is rising. I know he's busy, but he will eventually take a break, and then he can get his own #S@&%* garbage bag!

Fortunately, however, before I go on a rant about liberation, it occurs to me that in fact, he may have no clue as to where to locate said item. And so instead I kindly say, without a hint of sarcasm, "Sweetheart, if I should die before you…let me show you where the garbage bags are kept."

I like to think we have a modern marriage, one in which responsibilities are shared. And in many ways, we do. For example, in matters financial, where my ability with numbers is limited to simple addition—with a calculator—I'm most appreciative that my darling is able to guide us through the big decisions.

But in matters of the household, despite my emancipation, I'm afraid we revert to more traditional roles. And when the time arrives that I must relinquish my role as domestic goddess, I do want him to be prepared. So, to ensure a somewhat easier transition, for I know that he will miss me terribly, I'm compiling a list of need-to-know items. As I am still very much here, l refer to it as my version of a living will.

IF I SHOULD DIE BEFORE YOU, LET ME SHOW YOU…

- how to load the dish washer
- how to sew a button on your shirt
- how to put the drawstring back in your sweatpants after you pull too hard and yank it out
- where we keep the light bulbs
- how to change a light bulb
- where we keep the dog food
- where to put the recyclables
- how to replace the ink in your printer
- where to look when you can't find your glasses
- where to look when you can't find the TV remote
- where to find a new tube of toothpaste or a fresh bar of soap
- how to order stuff on Amazon
- how to reboot the computer
- how to clean the lint trap in the dryer
- that there is a lint trap in the dryer
- that there is a dryer, and a washer
- where we keep the toilet paper
- how to replace the toilet paper

This list is by no means exhaustive. It is a work in progress, to be added to as other gaps in knowledge become apparent. I know this is not a happy topic, but there is a great deal of comfort in knowing that after I'm gone, my darling will be able to replace that used cardboard cylinder with a brand new roll.

Perhaps this essay will inspire other couples to compile a list of their own. I certainly hope so. In the meantime, while I am still alive, let me not forget to show him where the garbage bags are.

Women Who Pack
(and Men Who Don't)

G lancing up, I realize that my title is a bit ambiguous. The word "pack" can have many meanings, such as "a pack of gum," or a "Cub Scout pack." Or carrying a concealed weapon.

So let me state at the outset that the following is not intended to be a sequel to *Orange Is the New Black*, although murder could very well be one possible outcome of the clash described below.

The "pack" to which I'm referring is "pack" as in "packing." Like putting clothes into a suitcase or a garment bag, or loading boxes into a car.

What has caused me to ponder the subject of packing at this particular time was our typical month of May sojourn from the south, back to the cooler north country, where we remain until it is time to once again follow the birds. We have been migrating thusly for the past fifteen years. The week before the departure is filled with decision-making about what we absolutely need to take with us, which is almost everything, and what can stay behind. Which is very little.

Then there is the physical act of actually *packing*, about which I get obsessively compulsive. And my husband? Not so much. So it unfolds that I am folding, while he will join me in just a minute as soon as he finishes writing his email. Which, as it turns out, is another version of *Gone with the Wind*.

This year however, circumstances were a bit different. I have developed a left shoulder problem, which has caused me less than full use of my left arm. And being left-handed… well, I don't have to explain. You get the picture.

So, about seven days before our departure date, I converse with the Master of Avoidance, and explain how, this year, I will really need his help. Which is my way of warning him not to even think about composing *War and Peace*. He is very understanding.

Fast forward to two days before departure date. Early morning conversation:

(Him) "I don't feel well. I think I'm getting sick."

(Me) "What's wrong?"

(Him) "My throat is scratchy. I think I'm getting a cold."

(Me) "No, you're not."

(Him) "But my throat…"

"But my shoulder," I remind him, as I hand him a lozenge, and point to the suitcase.

Looking for commiseration, I shared this story with a friend, who, in return related her story about how her husband managed to become bedridden for three different moving events. Listening to her, I am reminded of another friend, who has also complained about her husband's active nonparticipation when it comes to physical chores.

Can this phobic response to schlepping among cohorts be just a coincidence, or does it point to something more significant?

Armed with this anecdotal research, I have dared to form a hypothesis which, I admit, requires more supporting evidence. I believe that the inherent drive to disengage from chores such as those described above may very well be genetic in nature, and data collection to back up my theory may very well have to begin with referencing the Bible.

During the time of Moses, when the Hebrews fled from Egypt, who do you think did the packing? No wonder there was no time to let the bread rise. The women were too busy filling burlap sacks and loading them onto camels. And I'm pretty sure it was Eve who packed when she and Adam had to leave the Garden of Eden. Given the amount of clothing, it was probably just a small overnight bag.

So, to my female readers, if you have a story about a spouse with a psychosomatic response to packing or other physical chores, I'd be interested in adding it to my body of research. But it just may be that we're struggling against nature.

By the way, that cold never materialized, and emails were postponed until after the car was packed. That's the good news. We have arrived, and so has the car, which now has to be unpacked.

Has anyone seen my husband?

Husbands in Cars Going to Costco
(with apologies to Jerry Seinfeld)

I t is common wisdom that men, especially men of a certain generation, do not like to shop. In fact, a British survey of over 2,000 people found that men became bored after only twenty minutes of shopping, while women could go for a full two hours. This should come as a surprise to no one, at least not the people I know.

Recently, however, in sharp contradiction to the above findings, my husband has developed a timeless enthusiasm for browsing and purchasing. He's like an explorer who has discovered a new world. And the natives call this new world, "Costco."

I suppose the existence of three dozen pairs of sports socks spilling out of his drawer and the 64 oz. jar of mayonnaise in the pantry are really all my fault. I was the one who originally joined, although I can't remember why, and brought my darling along as a secondary member. Little did I know I would be creating a card-carrying Shopzilla!

For several years, the little piece of plastic, complete with photo I.D., did sit, unused, in his wallet. The turn-around occurred after reading an article in *The New York Times* which stated that Costco had very good value on hearing aids. Finally acknowledging that he did, in fact, have just a teeny bit of difficulty hearing (either that, or I was developing a stutter, evidenced by the repetition of most of my utterances), he decided to find out for himself if *The New York Times* was right.

Releasing the card from his wallet for the very first time, he gained access to, not just hearing devices, but to the 8th Wonder of the World, an enormous warehouse dispensing giant-sized products at discount prices. He was like Charlie let loose in the Chocolate Factory, as rewritten by AARP.

I knew I was in trouble when he returned from his first hearing test carrying the tallest bottle of vodka I had ever seen. "Are we entertaining the Russian Embassy?" I asked, making no effort to mask the sarcasm. He was unfazed and clearly triumphant. "Do you know what I paid for this? It was such a bargain."

"Great," I said. "I hope you saved enough to pay the carpenter to enlarge the liquor cabinet."

On the next trip to Costco for the hearing aid fitting, my honey discovered that this seemingly cold and cavernous entity had a nurturing side. This was revealed to him as he ate his way through the store, tasting food samples of every variety, culminating with the best hot dog with all the trimmings he had ever eaten. This and a bottomless cup of diet soda for only $1.59. Imagine! He considered having dinner there the following night, but was disappointed to learn they didn't take reservations.

Rushing home after his hearing aid adjustment trip, he couldn't wait to tell me his latest find. Costco sold books. Tables and tables of books. Best sellers at excellent prices. Judging by his level of excitement, I figured I had better call the carpenter again. We were definitely going to need more shelves.

His subsequent trips (was it my imagination, or did his hearing aids need an inordinate amount of adjustment?) brought further exciting revelations. Cartons of paper towel and toilet tissue now filled my garage. "It isn't food; it won't spoil," he rationalized. True, but would we actually live long enough to use all that paper? I could ask the same question about the socks.

The barbecued chicken he brought home for dinner one night looked like a GMO experiment gone haywire. I had no idea chickens grew that large. Did he forget the family wasn't visiting for another two months? I had to admit, though, that this Amazonian-sized fowl tasted good. Other food items would follow. Packages of steaks now occupy my freezer, and in the fridge, large containers of various spreads that could be used to cater a wedding. These, I fear, will eventually spoil long before my grandkids are ready to walk down the aisle.

"Like these pants?" my husband asked the other day. He had just returned from yet another hearing aid recalibration. "Yes," I replied, "and they fit well. "Costco," he proudly exclaimed, as he cut up his credit card for Saks. "I think next time I go, I'll get a few more pairs." Remind me to tell the carpenter that we need more closet space.

Like a true disciple, he has felt it a duty to spread the gospel. He has directed several of his friends to Costco's hearing aid department, and in doing so, has exposed them to the bounty therein. It is not unusual to overhear a conversation between my husband and one of his cronies, as they fondle a giant-sized bottle of scotch, in which they discuss how much more it would have cost if they had shopped retail.

So move over to the slow lane, Seinfeld. Coffee can wait. Because husbands in cars going to Costco will not be stopped.

The Insomnia Games

I am not, by nature, a competitive person. If I even so much as win at a game of Scrabble, my inclination is to leap over the board, hug the loser, and say, "sorry." Yet, each morning, upon opening my eyes, I find myself engaged in a verbal duel.

I'm not exactly sure when this all began. Perhaps it started on that critical birthday. The one when my bladder decided to stop cooperating with my need for hydration, and instead began taunting me during the night in two-hour intervals. Which I think is very spiteful.

I'm reminded of my former dogs. When they were old, I had to remove their water bowls no later than 5:00 PM to prevent them from awakening after bedtime because they had to go outside to pee. At least I don't have to go outside, but I'm definitely considering rolling back happy hour.

What is referred to as "a good night's sleep" has become elusive, as it has for my husband, who swears he hasn't slept through the night since he was ten months old. His parents are deceased so I cannot confirm or deny this report, but I do know that another factor in my *sleepus interruptus* is the glow of his iPad at some ungodly hour.

As a result of this pernicious insomnia, we have become quite competitive, constantly challenging each other as to who has had the worst night. A typical morning conversation might go something like this:

"How did you sleep?"

"Terrible."

"Yeah, well, I slept worse."

"I woke at 3:00 AM and haven't been to sleep since."

"No you didn't. I saw you. You were sound asleep."

"I was just pretending."

"So how come you were snoring?"

"I had to go to the bathroom three times."

"I had to go four."

"Yeah, well, I had leg cramps."

"I know. I heard you marching around the bedroom."

"No you didn't. You were sleeping."

The verbal jousting is halted by the current dog, who is covering his ears, and our need for coffee. This requires one of us to leave the bed, usually me.

I'm quite sure that competitive not-sleeping isn't limited to us. I believe we have entered a stage in life where sleep deprivation may very well be the new status age-related deficit, edging out other contenders, like who has the greatest number of body part replacements, who knows the best doctors, and who has the best HDL scores.

Conversations around a dinner table often focus on the virtues and pitfalls of choosing Ambien over Lunesta, or how spraying lavender on your pillowcase is very soothing and will lull you to dreamland. I tried that. I wound up with a damp pillowcase and an allergy attack.

And don't ever complain to a friend that you're tired all the time because you average only four hours of sleep. Sympathy will not be forthcoming, but rather, "You think that's bad? I *never* sleep."

As for me, I'm tired, and would like to withdraw from the game. I'd gladly relinquish the gold medal in exchange for a few nights of sound, solid, restful sleep.

And when my husband laments in the morning about how bad the night was, I would gently pat his hand, commiserate, and try my best to refrain from gloating. After all, I'm not a competitive person.

YOU'VE COME
A LONG WAY, BABY!

Old Ironsides

At first, I wasn't sure why my mind wandered to this particular topic. It might have been the sense of torture brought on by endless exposure to political gurus. Or perhaps it was the stomach ache which followed an uncontrollable fit of laughter. The latter occurred as I was perusing the latest issue of *The New York Times Style Magazine*, wondering, as I always do, "Who wears these things? And why?"

The giggling, which started slowly, was inspired by a photograph of a slender young thing (aren't they always?) wearing a corset, repurposed as a fashion statement, which could be yours, courtesy of Prada, for a mere $1K.

Or perhaps it was a combination of the two. No matter. Both result in pain.

In all fairness, it was the picture of the corset, and not cable news, that was the real trigger. Youthful memories came rushing back, and I was suddenly reliving the visceral discomfort caused by a diabolical undergarment known as The Girdle.

Ah. The girdle. I hadn't thought about a girdle in decades. And why should I? Better it stayed buried, along with other unpleasant repressed memories, like the angst of being the last girl on my block to need a bra.

My mother grew up in the era of elastic bondage when fashion required a rigid, controlled figure. She became a strong advocate for the girdle, believing that, in addition to its cosmetic rewards, it was necessary for improving and maintaining one's health and as a prevention against obesity. "It holds everything in place," she told me.

As girdles were not required under school clothing, but were an absolute necessity when one got "dressed up," I'm sure I sat in my classroom imagining that my liver, kidneys, and other internal organs were relocating at will inside my body, and that my stomach was threatening to expand with each exhalation.

However, Mother, like most women of her generation, wore a girdle every day. In the forties, as you will recall, most women wore dresses or skirts and stockings on a daily basis. How else was one to hold up stockings if not for those garters which dangled from the bottom of the corset?

I sympathetically remember my mother's girdle, or corset. It was a tortuous-looking garment that was held together by a series of hooks and eyes, and just in case you could still manage to slouch just a little, it was made stiffer still by plastic or metal stays, called bones. The corset, once in place on her body, was then hooked to her bra, as one final warning that anything less than military-style erect posture was unacceptable. No wonder my mother, by day's end, was incapable of smiling.

The girdle she deemed appropriate for my health and well-being, let alone containing my "baby fat" was somewhat less restrictive. It was a pull-on elastic garment, and although boneless, still felt very much like a sausage casing into which I stuffed my body.

And the baby fat? It wasn't hidden. Merely redistributed.

I would dutifully wear my girdle and stockings on Friday nights, when my friends and I would don our nicest dresses and go to parties. If I were lucky and a cute boy asked me to dance, I prayed his hand would not wander too far down my back where the stomach fat was pushed up above the waist, just enough to form a perfectly matched set of love handles.

And men, if you've ever had the occasion to run your hands over a woman's girdled body, instead of feeling soft and curvy, I can only imagine that it must have felt like caressing a building.

But I'm sure on those Friday nights, my mother's mind was at ease regarding her daughter's chastity. Even a seventeen-year-old couldn't maintain an erection for the time it would take to extricate a fair maiden from her undergarment.

Sometime in the late fifties or early sixties, girdles disappeared as a required piece of underwear for proper young ladies, and instead, stockings were held up by garter belts, which was similar to wearing suspenders around your waist. Guys, no matter what you think, this is *not* sexy.

Thus, there was a great sense of liberation when God invented panty hose, which I regard as almost definitive proof that She is a woman.

Today's female, fortunately, has more choices. As one forever scarred by my early girdle experience, I choose the "let it all hang out" approach. If a dress requires a restrictive undergarment, I simply buy a different dress.

But for those women trying to keep it together, there's always Spanx. Or, if you happen to have a spare thousand, Prada may just be your answer.

Errands "R" Us

Story ripped from the headlines: "Woman Found Safe in Her Vehicle After Failing to Return Home for 48 Hours. Claims She Was Just Running Errands."

When interviewed, Mrs. X said she didn't know what all the fuss was about. "This was just my normal schedule, except my to-do list did not go as smoothly as planned, is all."

Does my fictitious lady sound familiar? Someone you know? You? Definitely me. Especially on those days when I find myself getting in and out of my car so frequently that it feels like interval training.

Let's face it. Equality between the sexes stops short when it comes to errands. It is part of the unwritten contract between men and women that females still bear the primary responsibility for ensuring we never run out of toilet paper. Males will assist when called upon, but generally consider it a favor, as opposed to a part of their job description.

That's okay. Men have equally irksome things to contend with, like locating items of food in the refrigerator. (You're familiar with that cry, "Honey, where's the…?")

Errands aren't so bad. One or two, maybe. But then there are the days when the list seems to reproduce faster than you can scribble a check mark. And you fear that you will never see your home again.

One such day loomed before me very recently. But I decided I would not suffer the same fate as our female alter ego, Mrs. X. I would sit down and strategize. I would develop a plan of action that would outsmart those that might ruin my entire afternoon. With the focus of a cartographer, I would map out a route that would minimize time spent and maximize efficiency.

If I first dropped the dog off at the groomer, then drove to the car wash, I would be able to hit the post office and the pharmacy without backtracking more than two blocks. I could then go to the dry cleaners to fetch the white shirt my husband needed for the party we were to attend that evening.

Next, I would return the book to the library, bring the vacuum cleaner to the repair shop, buy some pet food, and stop at the stationer, all in a nice, straight line.

Executing only one right turn, I would be able to return the sweater that I bought on an impulse (why did I think I looked good in puce?), fill the car with gas, circle around to the supermarket, load the groceries, fetch the dog from the groomer, return to the pharmacy to pick up the prescription, and finally head back.

With a little luck, and not too many red lights, I should be home in an hour and forty-five minutes. Possibly a new world's record for errand-running!

Armed with my map, and filled with confidence, I headed out, dog in tow.

Items one, two, three, and four went without a hitch. Almost. I was somewhat thwarted at the post office by the woman ahead of me who was having some difficulty choosing the perfect postage stamp. It was a toss-up between the seasonal "spring flowers" or the traditional, patriotic American flag. While I commiserated with her about her dilemma, I was in danger of being thrown off schedule. I tried to ignore her murderous expression as I encouraged her to get on with it.

But the real snafu occurred when I entered the dry cleaners. I was brandishing my pink ticket and the precise amount of money, anticipating a quick pick-up, only to be told that the shirt was not yet ready. Could I please come back in an hour?

What? How was this possible? This was a disaster. This extra hour could disqualify me from the *Guinness Book of Records.*

A quick decision was in order. Do I abandon the shirt and convince my husband that he looks much better in light blue? Or do I add another stop to my list and buy him a new white shirt for the occasion? That might be more efficient than returning to the cleaners. But what if they didn't have his size and the trip to the men's shop was simply a waste of time? It was a risk I would have to take.

I returned to my car and reconsidered my destinations. The GPS in my brain was calling out for route recalculation. There was still the library, vacuum cleaner repair shop, pet store, stationer, sweater return, gas station, supermarket, groomer, and drug store.

I decided the shirt store could best be managed after I returned the sweater. This would require doubling back only half-a-mile, crossing the railroad tracks twice, hopefully missing the freight train each time, and resuming the rest of the journey heading northwest. Go! (In retrospect, I suppose I could have called my husband and told him to pick up his own damn shirt, but quite frankly, at the time, it never even occurred to me. Which tells me just how programmed I am for errand-running. Scary!)

Devoid of library book, vacuum cleaner, and sweater, and armed with a new white shirt, pet food, medication, a full tank of gas, and groceries, I finally arrived home, breathless. Only fifty minutes off schedule. Not exactly a world record. Yet. I would do better next time.

I was greeted by, "Hi. What took you so long? I thought you had left home (chuckle, chuckle)." I looked around for a heavy object. He was saved by his offer to help me unload the groceries from the car.

I was just about to store the last can of tuna, feeling very happy to be home, when a simple question sent me into a tailspin.

"By the way, honey, have you seen the dog?"

The Right to Bare Arms

O verheard at Saks:

Shopper One: "Ooh, that's such an adorable dress."
Shopper Two: "So why don't you try it on?"
Shopper One: "Are you crazy? It's sleeveless!"

As we approach the warmer weather, I am convinced that this scene will be replayed over and over again in boutiques and department stores across the country. I don't know if this fixation transcends continents, but American women of a certain age have a thing about their arms.

Typically, it is not the entire arm. The arm between the elbow and the wrist may be entirely acceptable. It is the area that lies between the shoulder and the elbow, otherwise known as the upper arm, that is the offending body part.

This female upper arm obsession was brought into sharp focus the other night when I was having dinner with some women friends, all contemporaries. Somehow the conversation became rerouted from the threat of global warming to apparel without sleeves. At the time, I wondered how we got from one topic to the other. But in retrospect, I can see a certain logic to this detour.

One after the other, my friends related how they long ago decided it was not in their best interest to display their upper arms. When even the most petite among us claimed that she was starting to feel bad about her elbows, I knew that this fixation had gone way too far! "OMG," I thought. "Upper arms have become the new neck!"

As the only person at the table who still dared to go bare, I could sense seeds of doubt scattering through my psyche. Was I seeing my own arms through rose-colored glasses? Or maybe one of those fun-house mirrors that make you look long and thin? (Every woman should have one in her home.)

Although I have been a dedicated triceps toner, perhaps the jiggly-Jello-look had finally caught up with me. I immediately reached for my sweater, and blamed my cover-up on the excessive use of air-conditioning, so common in South Florida establishments. And yes, wasn't it awful how they kept these places so cold?

Needing an objective opinion about the true state of my upper arms, I naturally turned to my husband.

"Honey," I said (I admit, I only call him honey when I want support rather than the truth), "what do you think about my arms?"

"Your arms? I haven't given much thought to your arms."

"My upper arms. Do you think they're in good shape?"

"As compared with who?"

After correcting his grammar, I recounted the conversation at the dinner table. He made an enormous effort not to laugh, patted my shoulder, and told me I had nothing to worry about. Once again, the term of endearment had yielded the desired result. But I quickly turned to make sure the shoulder pat had not triggered any excess fatty tissue disturbance.

So, as older women we hate our upper arms. But it doesn't stop there. I bet we're not too crazy about our knees, either. Summer's coming. That's when we all get seasonal affective disorder. Every time we put on a bathing suit, we each have an opportunity to hate our entire body. I don't know about men, but women have a tendency to be very hard on themselves. We carry around criteria for perfection based on some long-ago, presently unachievable body image. Hey, why can't I just say, "My arms look great for my age," and be satisfied with that?

But there are some braver souls among us.

I was in a clothing store the other day and, because of my recent obsession with upper arms, noticed this very attractive "older" woman. She was of medium-height, not particularly thin, with beautifully styled gray hair. Her make-up was well-applied, she wore interesting earrings, and yes, she was sleeveless!

Believe me, she would not be hired for a deodorant ad, or any other product requiring one to bare their arms, but yet, there I was, admiring her appearance.

"Good for you, lady," I thought. 'It's a hot day. Why not?"

And so, Michelle Obama, don't get me wrong. I truly admire you. But you have set a standard for upper arm fitness that few of us can match.

Therefore, if Hillary makes it to the White House, I'm sure looking forward to her rolling up her sleeves!

First published in May 2014

Are There Outlet Malls in Heaven?

On a scale of 1 to 10, with 1 representing the least likely to be overheard, and 10 representing the most likely, how would you rate the following query: "Hello, Irving, this is Stanley. How would you like to meet for lunch and then go shopping?"

Off the chart on the low end, I would suspect. But what if we substitute Carole and Rose for Irving and Stanley? I can hear the door slam as Carole heads for her car to rendezvous with Rose at the food court.

Women love to shop. Men? Not so much. Yes, there are a few of us who claim to hate it, and flaunt a sense of superiority at being less frivolous than the rest. But dangle the temptation of a 50% off sale at a trendy boutique, and let's see who's the first to hail a cab. This trait is nothing to be ashamed of. I would even go out on a limb and suggest that women's love of shopping is a biological imperative: a vestige left over from more primitive times when men were hunters, and women were gatherers.

If we examine the act of gathering, we will see many parallels with modern-day shopping. Women would leave their village in groups, chatting and socializing, and go into the forest or jungle in search of the best edible plants. There they would part grasses, push back branches, take their time, go from tree to tree, examining, checking, until they were satisfied with what they placed in their baskets. And they would feel a sense of satisfaction and accomplishment when they returned to their huts with their bounty.

We need not analyze too deeply to see how this translates to a trip to Saks with a friend. And, while we are no longer required to part grasses and push back branches, the motor memory of these actions surely enables us to deftly part hangers on pipe racks.

Men, on the other hand, often stalked their prey alone, and in silence. This highly focused pursuit is perhaps why men *buy*, but women *shop*.

A man might go into a store if they need something, like a pair of socks or a new shirt. They will spot their targeted item, buy it, and leave. Women love to take their time and browse, looking here and there, lifting a sweater off the table to see if there's a better one underneath. The modern-day equivalent of foraging, I suspect.

And, women tend to shop whether they need something or not. In fact, if you are fortunate enough to have some disposable income, "need" is a four-letter word. It has little to do with the experience.

Women who are true recreational shoppers (and that is most of us) find it very hard to resist the lure of the fashion outlet mall. It beckons to us like a siren's song. The anticipation of finding a deal at a high-end store produces something akin to an adrenaline rush. Besides feeling like you've discovered the Holy Grail, a bargain also comes with bragging rights. "Did you know that this blouse originally sold for $500, but I paid only $75? And if I don't raise my arm more than three inches, no one will even see the little tear on the right side."

Do we really believe all those claims about original prices, and the five subsequent markdowns that appear on the tag? Not really, but why spoil the fun?

And what about the fact that this was last year's dress? So what? Was last year so bad?

Truth be told, a good deal of what is sold at outlets like Saks Off Fifth, Barney's, and other high-end retail shops are not the real thing, but goods made for discounting. But among the inferior merchandise are the authentic deals waiting to be discovered by the sharpest among us who have honed our skills in the forest. There is treasure among the trash, and that's what keeps us coming back.

As for me, I will shop 'til I drop. Or as long as the stamina holds out and I continue to believe that trying on clothing for several hours burns as many calories as being on the treadmill. And in the end, who really knows what the afterlife holds? I'm not sure if there are shopping malls in heaven.

But in the event that there are, and I decide to be cremated, please scatter my ashes in Neiman Marcus Last Call.

Silver Lining

S o the other day I was on the phone with my friend Doris
(not her real name). She's had a very rough winter. Some
strange malady has been sapping all her energy. The slightest
household chore sends her crawling to the sofa to lie down.
Her doctors have assured her that it is nothing life-threaten-
ing, yet they can't seem to get to the bottom of what ails her.

I call her regularly for updates on her situation. Sadly, she
reports about all the things she cannot seem to do, all the
dates she's had to cancel, how she suddenly feels very old
and vulnerable, how bored she is, and how she doesn't even
have the energy to eat. Her voice reflects her pathetic state of
being.

I'm about to shed tears on her behalf, when suddenly there
is a shift. With a noticeable lightness of tone that definitely
was not there before, she states, "...And oh, by the way, I've
lost ten pounds!"

Immediately, I experience a change in my own attitude.
The place where there had been empathy was now occupied

by envy. Her malady would pass, and she would be ten pounds lighter. Diet-less weight-loss. That is so unfair.

I confess to finding my response somewhat alarming. Envying my poor tired friend because she was spared the calorie-counting and endless trips to the gym? What did that say about me? Had I completely lost my mind, or was I merely a woman of a certain age looking for an alternative solution to "weight creep," those subtle, sneaky ten pounds that, with each passing decade, find their way to your middle?

And, suddenly, last year's pants just won't zip anymore, even if you lie flat on the floor and coax your large dog to sit on your stomach. Even two large dogs sitting on your stomach won't allow those stubborn pieces of metal to come together. (Women blessed with the thin gene, do you even know what I'm talking about?)

Wasn't there a condition that would work for me? Nothing serious, of course, but maybe a prolonged stomach virus, or perhaps some extensive dental work that would render me unable to chew?

I thought longingly of my first trip to Mexico, when, in addition to a sun tan and a pair of huaraches, I arrived home with some strange flora or fauna that had taken up residence in my intestinal tract. Despite the fact that medical tests did not discover any deadly organisms, my stomach had turned into a food processor with the button stuck on puree. A little inconvenient, but over the course of three glorious weeks, despite eating hamburgers *with* the buns, and the sides of fries, I managed to shed seven pounds. Perhaps I should call my travel agent.

I wondered, would a man react similarly? Or was this just one more example of an intelligent, well-educated, sophisticated woman worshipping false idols? Idols like

Victoria's Secret models, or half-naked women on *Dancing with The Stars?* (Truth is, even in my best year, I never looked like that.)

I know. This is the part where I should give myself a good talking-to. A lecture about aging with grace, accepting the new normal, loving my still lovely, if slightly heavier self, about not focusing on belly fat, enjoying my food, and perhaps even considering getting a new pair of pants. I've tried it. It doesn't work.

I do acknowledge, however, that it's completely insane to focus on bacteria as a means of weight loss. And so my thoughts turn to another sure-fire path to fat reduction that does not involve dieting and the gym: stress.

Yes, this had some immediate possibilities. In another week, husband, dog, and I would be relocating, leaving our place in Florida to move up north for the summer. What this means for me is a sudden onset of OCD with more than a touch of mania.

Since I compulsively feel that the house must be left in perfect order, I will frantically move about the place cleaning, washing, straightening, and organizing. I will run up and down the stairs with armfuls of clothes that need to be packed and shipped. Outdoor furniture needs to be moved indoors. I will lie awake at night creating to-do lists. Closets must be reorganized, and perishable food disposed of. I'll be exhausted by the end of each day, and realize that I have forgotten to eat. (Forgotten to eat? Isn't that what skinny people do?) By the time we are ready to leave, I will be bone-weary and sleep-deprived.

But, living through all this hysteria is guaranteed to shed a few unwanted pounds. And that, my friends, is the silver lining.

Dress Code

O n the whole, I think women are fabulous. But also a little crazy. I can say this because as part of the sisterhood, I have license to go where no man should dare to tread.

As a group, we are certainly better-educated and more independent than the majority of our foremothers. But occasionally there is a circumstance that makes me question whether or not we have received our money's worth from higher education.

Case in point: it was a cloudy lazy Saturday afternoon, and my husband and I had spent the day at home catching up on neglected chores. In the midst of changing light bulbs and discarding leaky hoses, I suddenly remembered that we meant to choose a housewarming gift for friends we were visiting that evening.

Since it was already late in the day, I began thinking out loud about where we could go expediently to acquire something nice.

"Well, there's always Neiman Marcus," I said, envisioning their pricey, but elegant, gift department.

"Okay," he said. "Let's go,"

Taking a quick survey of my sweatpants and sneakers, I responded that I couldn't possibly go to Neiman Marcus looking like *this*. I would have to shower, change my clothes, fix my hair, and apply makeup. I estimated that all of that would take too much time. So I suggested another store.

"And will you need a makeover to go to that store?" he inquired, not unreasonably.

"No," I said without missing a beat. "I'm fine."

He didn't have to respond with words. I could tell from all that head-shaking and his mocking grin that he thought I had gone too long without eating. Better to believe that what I had just said was caused by low blood sugar, rather than conclude his usually clever wife was losing her mind.

Apparently, my husband didn't share the feeling that a trip to Neiman's required a wardrobe shift, although he was hardly in his Sunday best. And his sneakers were, in fact, not as nice as mine.

How could I explain that these are the rules, that you could wear your sweaty gym clothes to go to Target or Home Depot, but not to Bergdorf's? And that these rules have probably been acknowledged by women since birth, maybe even since the womb.

In the late sixties and early seventies I lived on Manhattan's Upper West Side, a part of town that, at the time, was home to drug dealers and working girls, as well as former members of the Woodstock generation who were now getting married and raising families. The average street uniform was jeans, T-shirts, or long flowing skirts and cowboy boots.

This was all fine west of Central Park. But we were careful to shed the tie-dye when we rode the cross-town bus. Then, we wore our "outfits," which were the passports we felt were required to enter the rarified world of Bloomingdale's. Or Saks. As if matching shoes and handbags would raise our esteem in the eyes of the salespeople.

Unfortunately, retail intimidation is not something we tend to outgrow. In fact, I'm not sure it doesn't get more ingrained over time.

Entering a fancy department store or boutique seems to require the confidence that only proper attire can provide. "Hey," my carefully selected outfit cries out, "I can shop here. I'm cool." I'm qualified to peruse the racks of clothing with price tags that could otherwise provide a week's worth of food to a starving village. I have the American Express Black Card. (Not really, but they don't know that.)

I don't know if men in similar circumstances are governed by the same set of standards. Perhaps some are. But I would bet not nearly as many or as often as women. Don't get me wrong. I'm not suggesting that we should all head for the nearest therapist. In fact, I'm not suggesting that we change a thing. Only that we take a step back and laugh at ourselves a little, and go right on doing what we do.

How humiliating it would be to enter a fine establishment and not have an eager salesgirl approach with a bottle of store-label water. That's why we follow the rules.

Before and After

The other night, in a restaurant, my husband happened to encounter a woman he knew from high school days. This is not unusual. My husband frequently runs into people from his youth. In fact, I once wrote about this phenomenon, which never fails to amaze me. (See "State of the Reunion," page 6.) Growing up in a small town, his high school class had about 200 students, while mine, big city girl that I was, had about 900. Like I said, I run into no one.

But I digress. He introduced me to his former classmate, a very attractive woman who had to be my husband's age. Even if she was one of the smart kids and skipped a few grades, she could only be a couple of years younger. So we chatted politely (they chatted, I just smiled pleasantly and tried to look interested), then went our separate ways.

When we were seated at our table, my husband turned to me and said, "She used to be very pretty." What? Were we looking at the same woman? Had something gone awry with his new lens implants? The attractive woman I just met was very pretty. Right here, right now, in this very restaurant.

Of course, my husband was remembering a sixteen-year-old version of Dolores, whose name I changed to protect the VIC (Victim of Insulting Comment). The Dolores he recalled did not have laugh lines around her eyes, creases around the mouth, nor age spots on the hand he shook.

Come on. People get older. It's what they do. So why judge a woman's appearance by some outdated standard that clearly no longer applies? No seventy-something-year-old female is going to look like a fresh-faced cheerleader. Nor should they be expected to. And speaking for myself, I don't want to.

How often I have heard this "used to be" phrase applied, usually by a man, to an older actress who, in her younger days, was considered "hot." But if she has dared not to have boob lifts, Botox, or skin resurfacing (ouch!), she is cast aside. Why are they still idolizing the pin-up version, but failing to apply a different aesthetic today?

I know I'm joining the voices of all those who decry our youth-worshipping culture, but I find that frame of reference really irritating, both intellectually and emotionally. And I swear that my ire has absolutely nothing to do with the fact that I just had another birthday.

And speaking of birthdays, on which birthday does a woman stop looking pretty, or hot, or beautiful, and start looking "good for her age?"

Looking good for one's age. There's another expression that deserves some scrutiny. What exactly does it mean to "look good for one's age?"

Against what standard is the recipient of this compliment being judged? And, by the way, to say one looks good for one's age is hardly a compliment. Telling someone they look good should not require a qualifier.

If I am seventy-five and look good for my age, does that mean other seventy-five-year-olds do not look good? Does that mean that my cohorts are largely unattractive?

And today, what does seventy-five look like anyway? Certainly not like my daughter, but I believe somewhat better than my grandmother?

"Age-defying" and "anti-aging,"— two more phrases that deserve the "delete" key. If you take a moment to examine them, what are they really saying?

Short of dying, it's not possible for a human being to defy age. Nor should we be asked to. And to be "anti-aging" is just not realistic, nor politically correct. Some of the best people I know are aging.

There is beauty at twenty and there is beauty at seventy, and we cannot expect them to be the same. As we age, gray hair, a few wrinkles, and some extra pounds should not be regarded as a disqualifier for seeing someone as very attractive.

In fact, when I look at photos of myself in high school, while I do see smoother skin and darker hair, I also see an insecure young woman who was struggling to find an identity. The person looking back at me in more recent photos is definitely older, but she is also someone with confidence, style, and a strong sense of who she is.

Society is harder on women than on men when it comes to aging. And we have more to overcome to feel good about ourselves. Yes, it's true. Life changes our appearance. But "pretty" should not have an expiration date.

April Is the Cruelest Month...

April is a month that seems to inspire poetry. However, Chaucer, who praised April in his prologue to *The Canterbury Tales* would certainly not have agreed with the opening line of T.S. Eliot's famous poem, "The Wasteland," quoted above. But then again, Chaucer was not a woman who had to face the terror and humiliation of shopping for a new bathing suit.

Neither, I recognize, was T.S. Eliot, who nevertheless, with these five words, revealed a remarkable empathy for older women confronting the reality of the coming beach season. It is highly doubtful that this application of Eliot's words will be found in any serious literary criticism. This particular interpretation of their meaning is all mine.

For me, April is highlighted by a series of family visits, ending with the delightful company of our three youngest grandchildren, who are not so young anymore, and their parents. Spending a week with children in the warm April weather of South Florida means spending a lot of time in the water. Which means spending a lot of time in a bathing suit.

Up to this point in the year, I had managed very nicely to avoid the heartbreak of too many revealed body parts. The weather had been cooperatively cool and not necessarily conducive to swimming. However, in the spirit of participating in my grandkids' favorite activity, swimwear was definitely the dress code.

Oh, I do have a favorite bathing suit that I tolerate rather well. I bought it several years ago. It is one of those one-piece "miracle suits," designed to make you look ten pounds thinner. Or not. However, it manages to embrace my boobs in a manner which does not make me look like I require milking, and covers enough pelvis to avoid the need for a Brazilian wax treatment. While not particularly sexy, neither is it dowdy. Somewhere between Victoria's Secret and Talbot's, leaning heavily towards Talbot's. But much to my horror, one day during my week as Esther Williams (millennials—you can Google her or whatever you do to resurrect dead film stars), my no-fault, default swim suit developed a big, fat hole!

The meaning of this discovery did not escape me. I was going to need a new bathing suit. I think one has to be a female of at least middle age to fully comprehend the trauma inherent in this situation.

I postponed this most tortuous of all shopping experiences while I practiced holding in my stomach on a single breath for as long as possible. When I was satisfied that I could get an adequate result without passing out, I knew it was time. But first, I knew I had to tend to my hair and makeup. If I'm going to be made to feel my worst, at least let me look my best.

How does one choose a bathing suit store? We of a certain age are advised to look for a shop that has a "good fitter."

What is a "good fitter" you might well ask? In the vernacular of the bathing suit world, this is a woman who is experienced in minimizing fleshy breasts and muffin tops, and the myriad of other possible bodily flaws. She will navigate you past the rows of tankinis (too much midriff reveal), bikinis (too much everything reveal), and straight down the aisle to the one-piece suits with magical concealing properties, and the ability to lift and tuck. After all, she knows that you've had it with sassy and sexy. You just need one that fits!

As I perused the racks where no teenager would be caught dead, I listened to her helpful suggestions about necklines, pleats, solids, or prints. I stared at my choices in dismay. I rejected the flowery print which reminded me of a cloth for a picnic table I once purchased at Bed Bath & Beyond, and also decided to forgo the animal print, which I feared would make me look like a pregnant cheetah. Thus, as in life, in the world of one-piece bathing suits, you can't go wrong with basic black. I bravely entered the fitting room, armed with several variations of black swim suits in a size recommended by the fitter, which happens to be a size larger than any other clothing that I own. Great. Just keep heaping on the humiliation.

I stripped to my undies and began the try-on process. Yuck! What was I thinking? Next! Finally, there was the magic suit. It was cut just right, reduced the tummy, and camouflaged a variety of imperfections. But, I noticed, it was a little too big. Summoning the fitter, I triumphantly requested the suit in a smaller size. I waited ten minutes while she searched, and returned with the bad news that they didn't have another one. Sorry.

"Well, that's that," I thought. "I did my best. I'll just have to go home and continue to practice inhaling my stomach.

Besides, my grandkids have all left. I can postpone the unpleasant outing for another day."

There was, I discovered that same night, a bright side to this experience. While I was switching channels among the various news stations, I had the opportunity, or misfortune, of seeing each of our presidential candidates delivering their latest rant. What I would normally have found excruciatingly annoying, now produced a broad grin. Obsessed as I was with the events of the day, I imagined Donald Trump, Ted Cruz, Bernie Sanders, Hillary Clinton, even John Kasich, standing front and center, and each was dressed in a bathing suit. How's that for an equalizer? Why, it's almost poetic.

First published in April 2016

Now You See Me,
Now You Don't

I was in a doctor's waiting room the other day catching up on my magazine reading (see "Death, Taxes, and the Annual Exam," page 78), when the title of a particular article captured my attention: "The Disappearance of Older Women."

Had this been in the *National Enquirer*, I would have assumed that it was another story about alien abductions. But why aliens would want to kidnap post-menopausal females was indeed a mystery unto itself. Perhaps on some planet not yet discovered by NASA they had overbuilt their assisted-living facilities? Even for the *Enquirer*, that seemed a little far-fetched.

As I continued waiting in the space designated for this purpose, I had ample opportunity to delve further into this article to discover that in fact it was a lament. Written by an attractive middle-aged woman (judging from her photo which may or may not have been retouched), she was somewhat bitterly expounding the fact that women, once they reach the age of fifty, become invisible.

Blaming this phenomenon on a youth-obsessed society, she went on to cite examples from her recent experiences which made her feel that she was no longer vital or important or noticeable.

She stated that men didn't look up when she walked into a room. She went largely unnoticed by passersby on the street. She could no longer hold the glance of a thirty-year-old man on the subway. Gone were her attractiveness and sex appeal, all washed away with the last flow of menstrual blood (my words, not hers). She believed herself to be in a slow, lingering decline.

Wow! Give that woman some Prozac, and save some for me. This was indeed very serious. Had I, too, become invisible but was too busy being busy to notice? I tried to recall the last time I had walked past a construction site to the sound of catcalls emanating from under the hard hats. Many years ago, probably, and even then, I recall he was a good deal older and most likely had cataracts.

As I checked more deeply into this phenomenon, I discovered not just other articles on the same topic, but also actual studies proving that women of a certain age shared this sense of becoming invisible. And it seems that the primary cause is that men no longer acknowledge us. If this is true, how sad that our self-esteem is so dependent upon male attention. But nevertheless, I think I might have discovered at least a temporary antidote.

Older women: want to *not* be invisible? Want to be noticed by men, particularly younger men? Then wander through the cosmetics section of a department store, or stroll past a boutique selling expensive anti-aging products, and I promise you, you will get more attention than Megyn Kelly at a Donald Trump rally. This is what happened to me: we were enjoying a visit from our beautiful twenty-four-year-old granddaughter and her twenty-four-year-old boyfriend. (Should I feel badly that he didn't try to flirt with me, or ask me to run away with him?) I had taken them for a stroll on a famous shopping street in our town, noted for its beautiful architecture and unaffordable clothing.

Standing outside of one of the boutiques was a man, probably in his thirties, dressed in a suit, shirt, and tie, all of which were black. His hair was black, his skin was swarthy, and his face sported a five o'clock shadow, not the grungy, but the sexy kind. As we passed by, he spoke. An exotic foreign accent added to his sex appeal. I noticed all of this, but paid it little mind until I realized he was speaking not to my beautiful granddaughter, but to me! He laughed, he joked, he teased; he was utterly charming. He was totally into me. I was the opposite of invisible! I was a target. Next thing I knew I was practically yanked into the store, and seated in a chair. He whipped out an elegantly packaged tube of cream, which he proceeded to apply under my left eye. He extolled its magical powers, how it would instantly reduce the wrinkles and puffiness, giving me a much younger appearance. When he was done, he held up a mirror so that I might witness this miracle for myself. I compared my two eyes, and told him I preferred my right eye, as the skin under my left eye still looked the same, but was now greasy. He did not appreciate my humor, nor my lack of interest in his product. I was summarily dismissed. He stepped back outside to stalk his next invisible woman. Afterwards, I had to laugh at myself for enjoying this little bit of flirtatious exchange with a handsome "younger" man, even if he was trying to empty my wallet by selling me some ridiculously expensive products that falsely promise to make me look like my granddaughter's big sister.

So, would I trade the confidence and self-awareness that aging has provided for a few more whistles from a construction worker? Absolutely not. There's freedom in no longer requiring that kind of approval. And there is freedom in being invisible. Perhaps attention is highly overrated.

Eat My Face

L ast evening, while engaging in the usual pre-sleep beauty ritual, I dipped my fingers into the jar of night face moisturizer only to discover that I was about to use the last dollop. While this is not quite as tragic as being unable to zip the cocktail dress you were planning to wear to the holiday party, or as inconvenient as a colonoscopy, it was still cause for consternation. You noticed I specified *night* moisturizer. Needless to say, my vanity tray also holds a day moisturizer, under-and-over eye creams, and a lip smoother. Last time I looked, I think my ears were still sufficiently hydrated. Having a Dorian Gray moment right before one goes to bed is not helpful in ensuring a peaceful rest. The jar of nocturnal face magic would have to be replaced, the sooner the better.

If you're not concerned about fine lines and wrinkles (then you're either not a woman, or still too young for a bra), this may sound trivial. But trust me. Being in the market for a new moisturizer is no fun. First of all, I'm dealing with an industry that makes me feel bad about myself, and then wants my money. Second, the range of choices is so vast that I can liken it only to selecting wallpaper, which, until recently, I regarded as the worst domestic decision any woman would ever have to make. As I saw it, I had two options. (Three, if I added "Save Your Money: use Vaseline." But I've been too brainwashed for that.) I could simply replace the same product I'd been using. Or, I could gullibly fall for the claims of something new and different. And perhaps more expensive. I chose Door Number Two.

I astutely observed the advertisements and tried to digest the promises. Did I want to nourish and replenish? Reduce brown spots? Challenge skin fatigue? Eliminate dark circles? Glow? Look five years younger in four weeks? Make that three weeks, and I'm yours! I ruled out all of the jars that state they are anti-aging, since this is not my personal political inclination. I am definitely not anti-aging, and don't know why any thinking person would be. Considering the alternative, I'll take as many birthdays as I can get. So I wandered around the cosmetic counters, dodging the perfume spritzers and reading labels. Many of the ingredients were familiar to me—retinol, lanolin, placenta from Tibetan yaks, artichokes. Artichokes? Wait a moment. Was this Saks, or my local supermarket? It seems that while I was not paying attention, the new, secret beautifying agents in these creams and lotions was—food!

Product after product bragged that they alone had harnessed the age-defying properties of wheat germ, lemongrass, or the acai berry. Avocados, in addition to making guacamole, firm and tighten. Soy milk nourished. Honey smoothed. Vanilla extract and almonds penetrated the deep layers of your skin, so you not only became enriched and enhanced, but also smelled like trail mix.

"Well," I thought. "Why was I wasting my time? I might as well go home, make a big salad, and smear it all over my face!" I think it was the artichoke that got to me most. I could handle the thought of spreading something smooth and creamy on my skin, like honey or avocado, but an artichoke? Rough and pointy was not exactly the feel I was going for.

So I left the store in utter confusion, wondering about the world we live in, and was Ghanian Shea butter more effective than that which came from a neighboring country? And what, exactly, was an Olay from which the Oil was derived?

And did I really believe that a famous model-turned-actress looked as good today as she did twenty-five years ago simply because she used a particular French face product spelled with an apostrophe? The beauty industry has been so successful at preying on the insecurities of women, particularly women of a certain age, that even the most skeptical of us are willing to let go of our disbelief and credit cards for the promise of a more youthful glow and the final solution to sagging.

So I shall have to return to the marketplace to search out the perfect night cream. But for tonight, I might have to apply my day cream before bed, and hope that it doesn't further disturb my sleep cycle.

Or, I can look through my pantry. Perhaps the Fountain of Youth is hidden in the granola.

HOW DID I GET HERE?

Summer Is a Bummer

Admittedly, I'm not a big fan of nostalgia. My capacity for fondly recounting the good old days is about half a cup. Sure, I have pleasant memories of growing up in the forties and fifties, but I'm not about to initiate a petition for the return of Howdy Dowdy, or lobby the fashion industry to bring back poodle skirts.

And, while I do miss Archie and Jughead, I don't get sentimental when reminded of what the price of gasoline used to be, or that a movie ticket used to cost twenty-five cents.

While I pride myself on being a forward-thinking kind of gal, I must confess that the arrival of this past Memorial Day weekend (the unofficial start of a new season), and the hot weather did combine to trigger images of childhood, and a good, old-fashioned, unfettered summer!

Whatever happened to the summers of my youth? I really do miss them. I miss the anticipation of them: the arrival of June, the end of school, the extended hours of daylight, more time to spend outdoors.

While I still enjoy the extended hours of daylight, my appreciation is now more often from behind a screen door. Summers used to be carefree. Now they are hazardous to your health. It's hard to enjoy summer when you are repeatedly reminded of all of the risks that come with warm weather. How can I possibly find the same pleasures of the season when I feel I must carry my garbage to the outdoor bin wearing a hazmat suit?

When did summer become dangerous? Blame global warming or the thinning of the ozone layer, but daring to walk out the front door unprotected feels like extreme risk-taking behavior. Perhaps that's why I experience an adrenaline rush if I go to my mail box without a hat on. And the beach? A real downer. My inner child longs to run freely in and out of the water, and to build elaborate sand castles complete with moats. But my outer older person threatens with more age spots and/or a trip to the dermatologist if I don't remain under the umbrella.

Would I consider a drive in a convertible? Never. At least not until the sun goes down. And even with the top up, one is not safe. I've learned that bad rays can penetrate glass. Therefore, I'm seriously considering window treatments for my Toyota. And when it comes to applying sun protection, perhaps someone can help me with the proper protocol. Do I apply my sun block before or after I rub on my skin moisturizer? If I apply my moisturizer first, will that prevent my sun block from working? But if I apply my sun block first, will that prevent my moisturizer from plumping up my wrinkles? In any event, there are now two layers of lotion on my face before I even put on my makeup. It's no wonder that I walk around for the rest of the day feeling like a stick of butter.

And remember when mosquito bites were simply that?

Annoying little itchy bumps that would subside in a couple of days? Since malaria was not a serious threat for those of us growing up in Bensonhurst, mosquitoes, while never our friends, were not to be feared. And insects did not dictate how we dressed. But this summer I am told that I must be cautious about the Zika virus. I have been warned to cover up and use insect repellent. Tell me, do I spray this on before or after the sun block and skin moisturizer? One expert even suggested we wear mosquito netting to cover our faces. Hey, why not? It's the perfect fashion accessory for the surgical mask worn to protect us from air pollution.

And in the good old summertime, who ever heard of ticks? Ticks were a sound made by my grandfather's pocket watch. But I must also cover up and spray to prevent Lyme disease. So that's me, in 90-degree weather, walking my dog in an outfit that looks like I'm about to embark on a ski vacation.

Maybe I should invest in that hazmat suit after all. I wonder, is it a one-size-fits-all, and does it come in a choice of colors? I admit summer still has some pleasures. I do look forward to fresh-picked corn, luscious tomatoes, and juicy summer fruit. However, please don't mind if I graciously decline that outdoor picnic for the safety and security of a screened-in porch. But as I watch my grandchildren from said screen porch thoroughly enjoying their summer, and their mother chasing them with a tube of sun block, another thought occurs to me. Summer hasn't changed at all. I have. Summer has always had its perils, but to be concerned about them was the responsibility of the adults. I can recall my own mother's hesitance to venture out from under the umbrella when she reluctantly consented to go to the beach, something as I child I could never comprehend. Today, that shade-seeking grown-up is me.

Death, Taxes, and the Annual Exam

It has been said, by Ben Franklin, I think, that the only things in life that are certain are death and taxes. I've taken the liberty of adding a third item to the traditional twosome: the annual physical exam. A call from my doctor's office reminding me that another year has gone by is now inevitable. And at this stage of life it would be foolish to ignore the request to make an appointment, especially since I'm fiercely dedicated to postponing Certainty Number One for as long as possible.

I typically schedule my yearly physical to coincide with my birthday month. There's something poetic about combining the two occasions—the angst of being another year older with the anxiety over the state of my health. Although I do regard the annual exam as necessary, it is definitely not something to which I look forward. I'm not sure why. It isn't painful. And certainly not as bad as a dental appointment. Yet I would rather be home ironing my husband's pajamas. And I really dislike ironing my husband's pajamas. But that's a story for another day. Having just undergone this yearly ritual, I am still able to recall the gestalt of the experience. I realize this is time limited. So I decided to seize the moment, and through careful analysis, try to determine why this process isn't more favorably anticipated.

I've dissected the elements, and think I've gotten to the core of the issue. My conclusions are described below.

The Waiting Room

Nowhere is this term more aptly applied than when you show up, on time, for a doctor's appointment. Doctors keep you waiting. It's what they do. It's so universal that I'm convinced there has to be a course in medical school called "The Anatomy and Physiology of Overbooking," or "My Time Is More Valuable than Yours." Accepting this as a fact of life, I have chosen my doctors, not on the strength of their education, experience, or the fact that my neighbor, Mr. Cohen, swears that this is the *best* doctor, but on the quality of their reading material. Whichever office has the best magazines wins the privilege of copying my insurance card. (At least, this was my modus operandi until I signed on with my latest internist, who actually sees her patients at the agreed-upon hour. Therefore, I show up a half an hour early in order to read the latest copy of *Architectural Digest*.)

Weights and Measures

The nurse, usually the first person to escort you into the inner sanctum, instructs me to remove my shoes so she may ascertain this year's bad news regarding my height and weight. By now, I know from experience that these numbers no longer move in the desired direction. Is it any wonder that I dread the results? The outcome is rarely what I would like it to be. My defense is facing forward on the scale and informing the nurse that if she doesn't want to explain to the doctor why I've fled the exam room, she should keep the numbers to herself.

The Robe

I ask you, is there anything more humiliating than a hospital gown? You can hardly keep it together with those two little strings, particularly when you are told to put the opening in the back. Do this, and you have completely relinquished control. And as embarrassing as the cloth gown is, it's like a burka compared to paper gowns. Paper gowns are shorter, impossible to close, and crinkle when you move. They bring new meaning to the term "gap in medical coverage." Therefore, in addition to reading matter, I recommend inquiring about the gown material before selecting a physician. This caveat may not apply to ophthalmologists and podiatrists.

Taking Blood Pressure

This simple procedure should be more or less straight-forward. But there is something that puzzles me. Why does the nurse ask if I have a preference between left or right arm on which to tighten the cuff? Is it possible that one side of my body is more hypertensive than the other? I strongly suspect that this is a trick question, and there will be dire consequences if I give the incorrect response.

The Urine Sample

You'd think that after all these years, I would have mastered the art of peeing in a cup. I wonder, is there a woman out there who can gauge the precise location of the urine stream, so filling that little plastic vessel does not result in a wet hand? If so, I'd greatly appreciate learning the technique. Please send me illustrated instructions some time before next February.

Exit the Nurse

The preliminaries are over, and the nurse has done her part. She gathers her equipment, and prepares to leave the room. Her parting words? "The doctor will be in to see you in a minute." I wonder, does she derive some perverse pleasure from saying this? Does she leave the room cackling to herself? You know that this is going to be the longest "minute" of your life as you sit there in the chilly exam room, wearing only your hospital gown, which is opened at the back, wishing you were anywhere else but there, and wait. (Again, the exception is my current internist, who actually entered the exam room within fifty-three seconds. I timed her.)

Enter the Doctor

The doctor finally raps on the door and comes in, smiling and sincerely apologizing for making you wait. Your anger is helpless against so much niceness. He (or she) proceeds to check your body parts and then instructs you to get dressed and meet him in his office. He sits behind his big desk and delivers his spiel about the state of your health. The news is good and you're relieved. The inconvenience was worth it. Same time, next year. That's certain. (Incidentally, if you want the name of my doctor, you know, the one who sees you on time, has good taste in magazine subscriptions, and does not use paper gowns, you can forget about it. I like things exactly as they are. How do I know you're not one of those people who will get there first and tear out the picture of the must-have handbag from the latest issue of *Vogue?*)

Romancing the Crone

For those of you who have imagined me lounging by the pool for the month of August, that couldn't be further from the truth. In fact, I've been lounging on my screen porch, which is nowhere near the pool, and doesn't dictate that I wear a bathing suit. But I have not been idle.

As a matter of fact, I've been very busy pondering life, and how I might best find purpose for all those estrogen-free years that lie ahead. You see, I was a post-menopausal seeker, looking for role models for the third act of life. I refused to accept that gray hair, a few wrinkles, and five extra pounds of tummy fat somehow reduced my societal net worth. (Although I do admit that all of the above does give one pause!)

Although I have reached a point in life at which my age exceeds the speed limit, I am not ready to step aside. Surely I still have something to contribute. I had heard of cultures which revered older women. And it was in this enlightened realm that I discovered the Triple Goddess—

the representation of the three stages of a woman's life. The Triple Goddess! Where had she, or they, been all my life? I had blithely experienced Stage One: The Maiden, and Stage Two: The Mother, with a total lack of awareness of my inherent value. No way was I going to blow Stage Three!

The more I learned, the less I feared being discarded because I was an "older woman." True, there were certain things I could no longer do, like become a Victoria's Secret model. Not unless they added about six more inches of fabric to their panties, and two more cup sizes to their bra inventory.

But neither would I agree to be ignored or overlooked by a youth-worshipping society. I had discovered a place of honor. I would embrace Stage Three of the Goddess cycle, and live out my remaining years as a Crone.

A Crone! I heard you gasp. But let me reassure you. Not the crone (notice the small "c") as represented by the witch in Hansel and Gretel, but the beautiful and benevolent Crone who appears as Cinderella's fairy godmother, the problem-solver who turns mice into horses and pumpkins into coaches.

Okay, so I'm exaggerating. I really don't intend to mess around with plants and animals. But I will strive to become the authentic Crone—the honored third aspect of the Triple Goddess.

According to legend, the Crone is a symbol of self-value, and respect. She is venerated for her experience, judgment, and wisdom—and clearly, someone to turn to when you don't know the answer to Final *Jeopardy!*

To quote from one description of the Crone Goddess, she is "the wisdom-keeper, seer, healer, and midwife, whose knowledge is sought out to guide others during life's hardships and transitions." Cool. Although I think I can do without the midwife part.

I hope it's not too late for me. With all this guiding and healing to accomplish, I probably should have started "Croning" years ago. But I'm a hard worker, and have confidence that I can catch up.

I do have one question, though. Must I look the part? Does deciding to become a Crone require a new outfit? I'm sure Crones no longer wear gowns and tiaras, or carry magic wands. But must I let my hair grow, and purchase flowing robes? Or, will people take me just as seriously if I choose Not Your Daughter's Jeans and a T-shirt? No matter. The important thing is to make up for lost time and immediately get to work on developing my wise-woman energy.

I'm really looking forward to engaging in my new role. Since I'm a novice, I will begin in the safe bosom of my very own family, and maybe work my way out to a few close friends. I'll have to let them know that I'm available for advice-dispensing.

Do I wait for them to come to me, or do I take the first step? Should I tell my son that he should shave his beard immediately because it makes him look like a red-headed Smith Brother? Or do I tell my husband that the color of his favorite sports jacket gives him the appearance of someone with the flu?

I don't think so. Because a truly wise woman knows when to shut up.

Eye Opener

By any chance, do you to remember an old movie called *The Enchanted Cottage* starring Robert Young and Dorothy McGuire? It was released a long time ago, 1945 to be exact. If you don't remember it, please don't lie and tell me it's because you weren't born yet. I happen to know how old you are!

Anyway, in this film, Robert Young plays a disfigured war veteran and Dorothy McGuire plays a homely maid. The two marry, and as time passes, fall more deeply in love. Within the confines of the cottage in which they live, they begin to appear beautiful to each other.

Well, apparently, I had been happily living in an enchanted cottage of my own. At least until recently, when a terrorist disguised as an eye doctor blew the whole thing to smithereens!

You see (she punned), I recently had cataract surgery. "No big deal," I hear you saying. "Just another, inevitable part of the aging process. Everybody does it." So if everybody does it, why didn't anyone warn me?

My eyes are considerably older than I am. And because of this I had accepted the fact that my reading glasses gradually got stronger, and I eventually needed distance glasses for driving. And at night I had noticed that the headlights of oncoming cars had become more distracting. But I figured it was due to inferior workmanship.

So you can imagine my surprise, when, at my last eye exam, the doctor suggested that I consider having my cataracts removed. What cataracts? Who had cataracts? Had he failed to mention this before, or had I just not been listening?

Who knows for how many years these insidious little clouds had been gradually forming on the lenses of my eyes, and, unbeknownst to me, had eventually caused me to view the world in a gauze-like haze? A little inconvenient at times, but actually not unlovely. It was a little like a filter used on a camera to provide a mysterious, romantic ambiance. And because the change happens slowly, one does tend to adjust to it.

Nevertheless, I agreed to the surgery, one eye at a time. So my left eye was now younger than my right, resulting in both good news and bad news. The good news was that I could see much better. The bad news was—that I could see much better!

OMG! Would you just look at the kitchen floor! Where did all that dog hair come from? I mean, I was aware there was some dog hair from my two constantly shedding Labrador Retrievers I had at that time, but when did they start going bald? Since the surgery, I had progressed from running the vacuum every other day to every fifteen minutes.

When had the walls gotten so dirty? My new fashion accessories had become a can of Ajax and a wet sponge. And, look, the paint was chipping in the corner. And I wonder, what had caused the scratches on the bedroom floor? We really needed to consider whether it was time for a new paint job, and for having the floors redone. Or possibly moving.

Shove over, Morty and Lee. Adorable as you might be, it was my turn to do a Swiffer commercial. I, too, had been living in a fool's paradise.

But the excess of dog hair, dirty walls, chipped paint and scratched floors were only foreplay for the granddaddy of all shockers. The morning following the day of the surgery, my husband heard a blood-curdling shriek emanating from the bathroom. He sprang from the bed, probably believing that our bathtub had been occupied by an army of palmetto bugs. Even one of those creatures would call forth a vocalization that could land me a role in a horror movie.

A tub-full of roaches having a spa day in my Jacuzzi would have been preferable—the true source of the shriek was the face in the mirror that was looking back at me. Apparently, during the night, I had channeled the late Dorian Gray.

Who was this stranger? She did look familiar, but the Susan I remembered did not have those pouches under her eyes, those deep laugh-lines around her mouth, the sagging jowls, or a neck that Nora Ephron would definitely feel bad about. And where did all those freckles come from? (Were they freckles or something worse?)

As terrifying as it was, I couldn't take my good eye off that face in the mirror. Whoever coined the phrase "reality bites" should receive a Pulitzer prize. Truer words had never been spoken.

I've always been good in a crisis, so as calmness returned, I formulated a plan. There was help out there. I simply had to reach out to my friends who, because they had been dealing with signs of aging much longer than I, knew the best repair people.

Later that day, the swelling under my eyes did diminish significantly. Unfortunately, I can't say that for the rest of the issues.

In two weeks I was to have the other eye done. I could only imagine what additional imperfections awaited me. While it is miraculous, cataract surgery can be quite costly. Yes, insurance does cover the medical expenses. But even the best policies don't include coverage for house repainting, floor scraping, moving, or cosmetic procedures. So, in the interest of parsimony, I have considered an alternative to the costly cosmetic procedures. For the near future at least, I would choose my companions more selectively. I would hang out only with those friends who still have cataracts. That way, they would still see me through the slightly foggy, but highly complimentary filter, and together we could all return to The Enchanted Cottage.

Which, by now, could probably use a new paint job.

Failure to Print

Honestly, did I really need another reminder that I was old?

I thought I paid my dues this year with a few more wrinkles, deeper frown lines, a couple of extra sun spots, and a pair of eyes that now require glasses when I drive. Oh, and to appease my tummy, some new additions to my "never-again" list of foods.

So, did I have to suffer yet another indignity of aging, in front of a complete stranger, no less?

No, I didn't lose bladder control. I lost my fingerprints!

Let me explain how this came to light.

My husband and I had applied for the Global Entry pass that is supposed to make air travel a little easier. If you have this card, you can bypass the lines at security and Immigration by checking yourself in or out using a special kiosk. Whether this method is preferable to being escorted in a wheelchair remains to be seen.

In any event, since neither of us could justify needing a wheelchair just yet, we thought we would obtain these cards, and become official "trusted travelers." Part of the process of qualifying for this privilege is an in-person appointment at a U.S. Customs and Border Protection office. Our appointment was in Ft. Lauderdale, Florida, at a building adjacent to the airport.

(Not knowing exactly where it was, I entered the address into my car's GPS system and set out with every confidence that we would be easily guided to our destination. I should have known that the day would not be perfect when my GPS was flummoxed by all the construction at the airport, and had us driving around in circles for twenty minutes. But that's a story for another day.)

We were interviewed by a friendly, uniformed officer. (I think they're called "officers." Or maybe they're called "agents." I'm not sure. In any event, he was friendly.) We responded to the routine questions and each of us in turn had our pictures taken. So far, so good.

Also required was a set of fingerprints. I went first. Guess what? They don't use ink pads anymore. Instead, fingerprints are recorded biometrically using computers and a scanner. It's simple, really. All you have to do is place four fingers on a piece of glass and the computer reads your prints.

Reads *your* prints, maybe, but unfortunately, not mine!

The nice gentleman tried again. Then, once again. But neither my left or right hand would yield a set of readable, unsmeared fingerprints.

Naturally, I became concerned. Had I contracted some exotic disease that was slowly stripping away my identity? But then this formerly nice man tells me not to worry. "This frequently happens with old people." Old people!!!

Apparently, says Google, as we age, our skin loses elasticity. (Every woman knows that already!) The ridges that form our prints get thicker, the height between the top of the ridge and the bottom of the furrow gets narrower, so they are less prominent.

The problem was eventually solved by applying some lotion to my fingertips, which magically allowed the scanner to take its impression. The no-longer-nice man also informed me that I might have to apply some lotion to my fingertips every time I try to use one of the Global Entry kiosks at the airport. Otherwise, it may not be able to read my prints.

Great! My Global Entry card that was supposed to eliminate some of the stress of traveling has just added a new anxiety. Maybe I'll opt for the wheelchair after all.

I also learned from Google that the FBI website has instructions for taking fingerprints of elders and others with impaired ridges in the pattern area. So not only am I a member of the social security set, but I'm also part of a new subculture of people with impaired ridges.

But having this knowledge is not very helpful. I'm still left with the sorry news that I'm now an old person with one less distinctive feature, and wondering what comes next. And it is not particularly comforting to know that there are others like me.

Someone or something has played an ironic prank. Or else, why would time remove the creases from where we need them, and add new creases to where we don't? It saddens me that Mother Nature isn't perfect.

Either that, or she possesses a very wicked sense of humor!

Roughing It?

Is there an official start date for one's second childhood? I
don't mean the one that accompanies the onset of dotage,
I mean a time of life when you no longer feel silly about releasing your inner pre-adolescent. I urgently need to know,
because it's already June and I'm thinking about enrolling in
summer camp.

I never went to summer camp, and I'm tired of being left
out! "Left out of what?" you might ask. Left out of all the
screeching and squealing that occurs when we are out to
dinner with friends, and three out of four (that's me who's
excluded) discover that they all went to Camp Gitche Gumee
or Maka Laka or some other camp named after a fictitious
Native American tribe.

Then they start reminiscing about the lake, and the
counselors, and visiting day, and the food, and how they
learned to water ski. All that nostalgia about Color War and
gathering around the camp fire. If I'm really lucky, I'm treated
to a chorus of the good old camp song.

And I'm left sitting there, wondering if anyone wants to hear about how I spent my childhood summers under the sprinkler at my inner city neighborhood playground. Probably not.

Not going to camp is one of my biggest childhood regrets. Bigger than not going to Woodstock and getting all muddy and high. Bigger than not buying last year's Prada handbag at half-off half-off from Neiman Marcus' Last Call outlet store.

I almost went to camp one summer. I think it was Girl Scout camp, in fact. Yes, I was a Girl Scout. I learned how to tie knots and properly fold napkins for a dinner party. (Who gave dinner parties when they were ten years old? Who gave dinner parties in Bensonhurst, Brooklyn, at any age?)

I forget why I ultimately decided not to go. But had I known then that my decision at that tender age would condemn me to outlier status as an adult, I definitely would have packed my trunk.

But alas, I am no longer a girl, and I can't go back. I'm resigned to the fact that Color War was just not in my deck of cards. But that doesn't stop me from contemplating what a camp experience might be like at this point in time.

First of all, I would definitely need a lower bunk. The reasons for this should be obvious to anyone old enough to have second thoughts about changing a light bulb in an overhead fixture.

I don't mean to sound like a snob, but there would have to be cabins in which the toilets are en suite. The thought of trudging to an outhouse at 2:00 AM is about as appealing as a lukewarm cup of instant coffee.

Then there's all that sharing. Sharing sleeping space, sharing a bathroom, sharing a shower. The potential of seven other females seeing you naked.

I hope it won't turn out to be one of the camps where they drop you in the woods with two rocks and a toothpick and you have to make your own way back. I think the most rigorous survival experience I could handle at this point would be having to leave half of my skin care products at home.

Seriously, who among us could possibly endure eight weeks without face creams, body lotions, hair dryers, gels, or mousses? To say nothing of missing our appointment at the beauty salon for a trim, blow dry, and at least one process?

I think I would be game for all the activities. Activities are fine. In moderation. With frequent rest periods. Followed by a relaxing massage. And regarding those early morning swims, I would ask to forego the dip in the heart-stoppingly frigid lake in favor of a pool heated to just below body temperature.

Tell me honestly, you veterans, what's camp food really like? Will they have half-and-half for my mid-morning iced beverage? And will they provide Splenda or do I have to bring my own?

Funny, this entire concept is starting to sound less and less compelling. Reconsidering my current requirements, I have confirmed how foolish it is to contemplate a later-in-life camp experience.

But while one door closes, another door opens. The Golden Door that is. Clearly my time would be much better spent at a spa!

Daughter of a Beach (Hater)

The inevitable has happened. The insidious process has reached its conclusion. The final step has been taken, and the journey is over. I can deny it no longer. I have become my mother!

Despite our self-righteous cries as young girls that we will never be like *her*, one day we look in the mirror, and there she is, peering back at us. This should not be shocking. Certainly our own aging process was genetically designed to parallel hers. Mine started in my twenties with the appearance of the first prematurely gray hairs. Which, by the way, I used to pull out. But this only works for so long, unless you prefer bald spots to gray patches. So I stopped pulling and started dying.

Familiar patterns of lines and wrinkles begin to emerge. The threat of a double chin avoided with just a touch of liposuction. Recognizable facial expressions and gestures. You catch yourself in mid-sentence and realize that you are about to say something that is exactly what she would have said. Something you swore you would never say.

And the list of similarities goes on. But in my case, the ultimate surrender was The Beach! In my prior essay, I attempted to evoke your sympathy by revealing my deprived childhood and how I never went to summer camp. But there was compensation in the form of weekend family trips to the ocean.

My father was in charge of the food. He would cook roast beef and make potato salad, and start the sandwich preparation early in the morning. Coolers and jugs and beach chairs, blankets, toys, and towels would be loaded into the trunk of his latest used car. These were accompanied by hats and shirts, and changes of clothing. Heaven forbid we should get a chill from wearing our wet bathing suits. (Weren't bathing suits supposed to get wet?) We were embarking on a fifteen-minute drive to Coney Island with enough gear to travel the Alcan Highway!

I was happy. My brother was happy. I think my father was happy. The only one who was miserable was my mother. My mother intensely disliked the beach!

Her attitude was a complete enigma to me. And so contrary to my own. I was thrilled to be at the beach. I loved the sense of freedom. I loved the sun, the gentle waves, collecting shells. I loved playing in the sand and burying my brother, wishing I didn't have to dig him out.

My father seemed content. He swam, then relaxed and read the newspaper. And where was my mother while all of this was happening? Where she *always* was during these forays. Covered from head to toe and sitting under an umbrella. Occasionally she could be coaxed to wade in up to her knees, but after five minutes, she would scurry back to her hiding place. There was nothing about the beach that pleased my mother. She hated the sun. She hated the feel of the sun lotion. She hated the sand. She had a special facial expression that she reserved for when some of it got in her food. Sort of a cross between seeing a dead animal with its guts hanging out and biting into a lemon.

Her favorite part of the day was when it was time to go home. Then she could get into a shower and wash away all the gritty unpleasantness. Could this beach-hater be my real mother? I was convinced that I had been adopted.

When I reached adolescence, and could travel to the beach on my own with a group of friends, I think my mother ceremoniously burned her bathing suit.

My own romance with beaches did not end in childhood. Any opportunity to spread a blanket, I was there! Domestic beaches, foreign beaches, man-made beaches on a lake, it didn't matter. Beach vacations were the best. Despite being enveloped in total inertia, you could still feel like you were doing something. You were at the beach!

When my children were young, I took them to the beach, and once again, the trunk of the car was packed to overflowing with stuff!

It was always my dream to own a house at the beach, which we did for ten happy years. My own children grown, I lived my fantasy of walking with my dogs every morning and watching them joyfully take on the challenge of running through the crashing waves. It was back to being easy. Dogs don't require a lot of stuff! Then my husband suggested moving to Florida. When I could finally speak again, I told him that one of my conditions of doing so was that we must live near the beach. And so we did. But gradually the universe began to shift.

Now on the beach, you will see a woman, covered in protective clothing, with hat and sunglasses, sitting under an umbrella. She does not appreciate the sun and has slathered herself in sun screen. She fears skin cancer and more brown spots. She might venture into the water for a quick swim, but feels safer under the shelter. She hates how the sun screen causes the sand to stick to her skin. She tries to open a bottle of water and is annoyed that there is sand all over the cap. But for the sake of her husband, she endures. Finally, he's ready to leave, and she is once again happy.

This woman could be my mother. But it's not. It's me. The transformation is now complete.

Relaxation 101

So I just had another birthday. How do I feel about that? Since you only stop having them after you're dead, I guess I feel pretty good. In fact, I've recently made some serious investments in the future by electing to renew my car registration for two years instead of one, and my membership in AARP for another five. How's that for a burst of optimism?

But birthdays do tend to make one pause and take inventory. Of body parts, for instance. All in all, I'm not doing too badly. My knees still bend and I am able to navigate a staircase. Which is handy as my bedroom is on the second floor. My hips remain, as always, too wide, but the joints are articulating. My back? I'd rather not discuss it. Let's just say it's no worse. And I'm grateful that during the past year, gravity has not been too unkind to those anatomical structures that tend to obey Newton's law.

There has, however, been a slight change in my vision. My annual visit to my eye doctor resulted, for the first time, in a prescription for distance glasses, which he suggested

I use for driving. In an attempt at myopic humor, he also remarked that I wouldn't be able to fly an airplane without them. I dutifully laughed, and commented that this would not have a significant impact on my life. Nevertheless, just in case, I make sure to include them in my carry-on bag.

So really, I can't complain. (Well, I can. One can always complain.) I think I'm doing pretty well. For my age.

There is, however, something I would like to accomplish before another year flies by. Something that has thus far eluded me. Something that would add significantly to my quality of life. Or so I'm told. I would really like to learn how to relax.

After all, isn't this the time of my life when I'm supposed to be smelling the roses? Watching sunsets? Taking the time to let the dough rise? Yet I'm still telling myself that matzoh is just as good!

I envy my husband, who eases into the day by reading the entire newspaper. I tried that once. I think I got to page two of the first section, before I was overcome with restless body syndrome.

I would like to be able to sit outside on a beautiful day and read a book without noticing a plant that needed water, a weed that should be pulled, or dog poop that I neglected to pick up. And there I am again, a body in motion. Perhaps I should try reading at someone else's house, sitting by someone else's pool. Maybe if it was my neighbor's plant, I could just let it be. I doubt it.

Do you find manicures and pedicures stressful? I do. Although I'm embarrassed by my frequently naked toe nails, I am prevented from taking regular trips to the nail salon due to the fact that it requires me to actually sit still for a seemingly endless period of time. I barely manage to get through the soaking, scraping, sticking, trimming, and enameling phases. By the time I'm required to place my toes under that little dryer and sit for ten minutes more, I feel like a hyperactive child who's just been given an extended time out. (Perhaps I am a hyperactive child.)

Massages are definitely out of the question. Unless I find a masseuse who is willing to follow me around the room. Lying face down on a table with my head in a little circle for an hour or more is just not in my DNA. In spite of the dim lights, scented candles, and music that simulates water gently flowing from rocks into a beautiful, deep pool, I'm still dancing a jitterbug in my head. And all those water sounds do not do my bladder any favors.

I've already tried yoga and meditation. I was warned by the instructor that my constant wriggling was ruining the asanas for the entire class. Far be it from me to ruin anyone's asana. Besides, I'm not all that crazy about yoga pants.

Visualization was a disaster. I couldn't stop myself from conjuring dog poop. And when my mantra became "gotta go," I knew that I was licked.

I realize that I'm in serious need of reprogramming. Some type of behavior modification that will allow me to more fully enjoy the moment. So here's my plan: I'm going outside with a kitchen timer. I will set it for fifteen minutes and force myself to sit in a lounge chair until the timer dings. I will have a magazine and a glass of iced tea. I will read the article about seventy-three ways to look great after sixty. And no quitting after fifty-nine. All seventy-three! I can do this. I have discipline. Self-control. And I will not see that plastic bottle next to the tree that belongs in the recycle bin.

I will gradually increase my sitting time every day. I will abandon magazines and read a book. I will have a second glass of iced tea. I will not leave my chair to answer the phone or fold the laundry. I will sit still!

Why didn't anyone tell me that relaxing was such hard work?

Bowled Over

O n any given day, there are countless reminders that I am an old person. Not least of which is the pain in my lower back when I uncurl my body from the driver's seat of my car. There is also the fact that I now prefer to sit when putting on my panties, for fear that this will be the morning when my balance will fail me as I stand on one leg in order to insert the other leg into the proper hole.

When I ask for a senior ticket on the commuter train the conductor no longer questions my veracity. And did I know that Drake had a #1 single hit on the Billboard chart? So did Pink. And what was I doing when pop stars began economizing on names?

I've gotten somewhat used to the little age memos that life sends me on a daily basis. But every once in a while, I'm startled by the totally unexpected. Like checking into a hotel room and having the sensation that I've entered another galaxy.

It was a simple overnight stay at a hotel in New York. A hotel that I've always regarded as rather Old World and traditional, which was part of its charm. So you can imagine my surprise when I put the key, excuse me, key card, in the door, and walked into what could have been a movie set for *Star Trek*: Spock Takes a Vacation.

Forget about comfortable, old-world charm. This was twenty-first century millennial. The entrance area was black and glossy. And very dark. My husband (yes, he was there, too) and I groped the walls to find a light switch, which was a tactilely challenging activity. The familiar toggle or rocker was nowhere to be found.

Finally, the groping yielded an accidental result and an overhead light magically and gradually revealed a shiny black ceiling, and an equally shiny black floor. Everything was black, and shiny. And what wasn't black was gray. I guess Mr. Spock finds color offensive.

This was a room that should have come with an instruction booklet. At least for people born way before there was a Drake or a Pink. Every aspect of it was a technological wonder: a TV that rose from the foot of the bed, lights hidden in baseboards that magically sensed your approach and departure, and window shades that had no apparent means of being lowered. This was particularly disturbing, as bedtime was approaching.

Again, we groped the walls for a control mechanism with no immediate success. "What if I stand in the middle of the room, and recite Abracadabra," I suggested. "Or if that doesn't work, we could try the Sesame command."

Admittedly, I felt like an idiot. Should a hotel room make you feel like you've been transported from a nursing home into the future? We never did quite master the numerous functions of the panel that controlled the overhead lights. Fortunately, by some miracle, there was a lamp with a pull chain.

But the pièce de résistance, the crème de la crème, the icing on the cake, or whatever your favorite euphemism is for "over the top," was to be discovered in the bathroom. That was where I encountered the Smart Toilet.

I had heard about these clever potties, but never met one face-to-face, or should I say butt-to-seat? I entered the bathroom and Mr. Toilet uncannily knew that I was there. He automatically raised his seat cover, as if inviting me to sit. I admit I was somewhat hesitant upon noticing that the toilet was actually plugged into an electrical outlet. I imagined the headline: "Lady Fried While Emptying Her Bladder."

But sit I did. On a seat that was heated. It's 82 degrees outside. Is this really necessary? Mr. Toilet knew I was sitting on him, and all systems were activated. When the business was done, he flushed himself and lowered the lid. What? No robotic arm to tear the toilet paper and finish the job?

"Should I thank him?" I wondered, "Or maybe leave a tip like you do for a matron in a public restroom?" It's a sad day when a toilet can make one feel inept.

I have to say that after a while, Mr. Toilet became very annoying. His constant saluting was uncalled for. "Shut your maw, you stupid toilet. I came in to brush my teeth." Fancy that. Now I was talking to the toilet.

I'm now in the sanctity of my own house. I'm turning lights off and on with my toggle switch just because I can. And I'm left to ponder. Of all possible inventions, did the world really need a self-operating electric toilet? But perhaps I am being more than a bit behind the times. I'm sure there were plenty of people who thought outhouses were perfectly sufficient.

Nevertheless, owning one of these babies is not high on my list of home improvements. I never regarded the manual raising and lowering of a toilet seat lid as a burden one must bear, second only to drawing water from a well and carrying it up a hill in a wooden bucket.

But I shouldn't sell the inventor short. Perhaps he or she had found the solution to an age-old dilemma that has plagued dual-gender households for centuries: let's leave it to Mr. Toilet to determine the proper position of the seat.

Generation ?

It occurred to me the other day that I was invisible. Not just me, but my entire generation. It appears that we lack importance. I'm basing this rather sad conclusion on the fact that we have been entirely overlooked by the folks who bestow catchy cohort labels.

Let's get specific. At the risk of revealing my true age, which most of you already know, I'm referring to those of us born between 1926 and 1946. Admittedly, I have steel wool in my brain when it comes to math, but according to my calculations, we number almost 28 million (2010 U.S. census), and yet we go about our daily lives without a cultural tag. And personally, I'm feeling a bit resentful. What kind of legacy is this to leave to our children and grandchildren, otherwise known as the Xs and the Ys, and possibly the Zs?

Born too late to be World War II heroes, and too early to be a part of the post-war birth explosion, we have wound up sandwiched awkwardly between the Greatest Generation and the baby boomers. An entire generation without a context!

No doubt a result of having too much time on my hands, I decided to delve into this matter a bit further. Perhaps understanding the genesis of other generational labels would allow me to suggest something clever and catchy for my own. Something that would acknowledge the "nameless" 28 million. Something that might fit neatly as a crossword puzzle answer or a response to a question on a TV game show.

Well, thanks to Tom Brokaw, who happens to be one of the faceless, those born between 1901 and 1926 were widely lauded as the Greatest Generation. I don't disagree. They survived the Depression and fought the Second World War. They deserve the recognition, but come on, Tom, whatever happened to taking care of your own?

And the hype about the baby boomers? Aren't you just sick of it? Those born between 1946 and 1964 think they're so special. And who can blame them with all the attention they've always gotten from the media and the marketers. Big deal. So you've earned a lot of money and went to Woodstock. But you have no exclusive claim to rock 'n roll, civil rights, or feminism. Some of us latter-born question marks were right there with you.

Generation-naming just kept moving forward, leaving us further in the dust. Soon there was Gen X, a term with literary roots co-opted once again by Madison Avenue. Covering roughly the years 1966 to the early 1980s, the X originally meant that the fate of this generation was unknown. Gen Y was so-called because it was the next letter of the alphabet. These folks are also known as the millennials because the majority come of age after the turn of the century. There are actually more of them than there are boomers. But I'm getting a little sick of the attention they're getting, as well, with all the tweeting and Instagramming, and the me-me-me attitude.

But what else can you expect from a generation that wins ribbons just for showing up? All of that self-centeredness, however, does not make them ineligible for a unique identity, even if the word "millennial" does evoke visions of a multi-legged insect.

And have you heard about Gen Z, also known as iGen? Born after 2001, and most barely old enough for a bar mitzvah, they already have the attention of the cultural pulse-takers, while their grandparents and great-grandparents slip further into obscurity. All of which brings us to today, when I'm sure somewhere someone is working hard at predicting the zeitgeist of a generation yet to be born, and trying to figure out a catchy name.

So back to the predicament of the nameless 28 million. Surely there were significant events during our decades that would lend themselves to an overriding identity. For example, I've heard us referred to as the "depression babies" or the "war babies," but those are such downers. Certainly we can do better.

We are the generation that saw the end of prohibition, the New Deal, Social Security, Superman, and sliced white bread. (Forget the last one. I think I'd rather be known as a "war baby.") The truth be told, I actually discovered that my generation did, in fact, have a name. If you are not a sociologist, I challenge you to tell me what it is. I don't recall ever seeing it used in any type of popular media in my lifetime. If you were born between 1926 and 1945, welcome to the "silent generation." The "silent generation." How does that sit with you? Called thus because we didn't make waves, worked hard, and stuck by good old-fashioned values. All positive traits, I suppose, but so boring!

So as the silent generation, it seems fitting that we have gone unnoticed. And now that the truth has been revealed, however disappointing, perhaps it's time to move on to more important causes, such as discovering the true nature of Atticus Finch.

After all, "What's in a name?" asked Juliet, from her balcony in Verona. But at our age, should we really be debating existential questions with an iGen?

HOW TO COMPLAIN...

How to Complain When There's Nothing to Complain About

I knew this day would come. I've been dreading its arrival for over three years. It's that very disquieting sensation of tranquility, however temporary, when your existence has reached an unsettling plateau of comfort. And, try as you will, you just can't seem to find anything to complain about.

I know how enviable the circumstances in which I currently find myself may appear, but when you're engaged in a pursuit that requires kvetching, this situation is a disaster! It's humiliating. I am an embarrassment to my ancestors.

How could it be that my life has no respect for my deadline, self-imposed as it is? An essay is due, and I am gripe-less.

Feeling very much like Koko, the Lord High Executioner from *The Mikado*, I am in desperate need of a little list. So I begin to flip through my mental file cabinet for potential sources of irritation.

Let's see: last weekend we traveled north. Surely an encounter with an airline could yield all sorts of problems. But no, nothing, *nada*! The flights were on time, even early.

My in-flight TV set was working, and, to my joy, showing a *Law and Order* marathon. The man sitting next to me was not obese, did not have bad breath, did not try to talk to me while I was engrossed with my beloved Olivia Benson, and didn't have to go to the bathroom—not even once! Can things get much worse than that?

How about our outdoor dinner party? Certainly ripe for potential multiple tragedies. There was a whole host of concerns. We worried about the temperature. Would it be too hot or too cold? Wind gusts of 25 miles-an-hour or, no wind at all but plenty of little biting things dining on our guests?

Would it dare to rain? Would the intracoastal be at low tide so our company would have a perfect view of mud? And a possible odor of something akin to milk that had been accidentally left out of the refrigerator for a few days? Would a female friend in too-high heels trip coming down the spiral staircase from the upper deck, requiring a visit from the EMS?

But no, none of the above. Everything was perfect. Couldn't have been better. Food was excellent, temperature just right, fish were jumping and the water level was high. Slight breeze, no bugs. And not one sprained ankle in the group. Do you see where I'm going with this? I'm beginning to feel more than a little hopeless.

"Keep searching," I tell myself. "Something will come up."

The dry cleaner has not lost any clothes lately. No long lines at the bank. The person ahead of me at Starbuck's bought only a bottle of water. The supermarket did not run out of my favorite no-fat, sugar free, imitation chocolate fudgesicle. And there was plenty of Cool Whip.

The weather has been beautiful, the air reasonably dry, and my golf game, after taking a dive, has recovered to its accustomed level of incompetence. My appliances are purring, my computer is behaving, and I haven't scratched the car in two weeks. I'm not feeling fat, my bad hair days have been at a minimum, and a stranger in a diner told me I was beautiful. Can circumstances get any worse than this?

I suppose I could always complain about my children, but I have declared them off-limits. I may have to reconsider, however. It's starting to look like these are very tough times for a whiner.

I concede that this is not going well. That my quest for a societal offender is coming up empty. I have one last hope. I turn my thoughts to my spouse.

Yes, he still falls asleep gripping the TV remote in a tightly clenched fist, but that's an old story. As is his misplacing things, constantly giving me driving lessons, and messing up the house with papers. Good news, or in this case, bad news— he has lately limited his cooking to the outdoor grill so my kitchen has not been under siege.

Surely, we must have had an argument about something recently, or at the very least, a mild disagreement. But I can think of nothing. Maybe I'm losing my mind. Now that would be something to complain about, but I'll need more proof.

Perhaps the universe is trying to tell me to relax and appreciate the fact that for this brief moment in time, my stars are in alignment. It is a shaky peace at best, because we all know how quickly the axis can shift.

So I shall do just that, and be grateful that I am leaving the rest of this page as blank space. For now.

All A-Twitter!

I want to be perfectly clear. I know for a fact that I could have happily lived out the rest of my days without ever having participated in Social Media.

Social Media. I find the very name a paradox. Can you imagine anything more *anti*social than a system that causes one's complete attention to be focused on a device screen, to the exclusion of everything and everyone around you? *Hey, watch out for that manhole!*

But one must do what one must do, and when I initiated my blog almost four years ago, it was recommended that I create a Facebook page to reach a larger audience. There were hundreds, even thousands, of people out there waiting to "friend" me, hungry for every word I was writing. I have to admit it has worked (well, maybe not thousands) and that my heart does beat a little faster when I see another "thumbs up" icon on my site.

But unless you count the fact that I spread happy birthday wishes all over the Internet in response to those helpful reminders, posting my essays has been the extent of my social media involvement. Thus far.

Now that I have two books, in addition to the blog, perhaps further growth was in order. So I hired a Growth Professional, who, like my hair stylist, decided it was time for a new look. The old one was fine, but was a little dated. Sort of like me. The situation bore a resemblance to cosmetic surgery, in that neither service was covered by insurance.

Of course I wanted to be what was trending. Who wouldn't? So when the GP threw out such seductive terms as "repurposing," "branding," and "launching," I orgasmically said, "Yes, Yes, Yes!" But why in heaven's name do I need a Twitter account?

Despite receiving no satisfactory response to that last question, I nevertheless found myself logged on to You Tube watching a series of videos which might as well have been labeled "Twitter for Dummies."

One of the first things I learned is that on Twitter, you do not have "friends." You have "followers." Having followers certainly does give one a sense of importance. Look what it did for Jesus.

I also learned that in order to be identified when I tweet, I must have a "handle," a user name preceded by the "@" sign. And my topic, or whatever it is I'm tweeting about, must be preceded by "#," the icon formerly known as Prince. I mean, number sign or pound sign, now referred to as a hash tag.

Okay, so I have the basics, and I'm ready to begin. Now I've only to figure out what it is that I want to share with my followers. What messages do I want to give to the world at large? What essential observation, brilliance, cleverness, wisdom, wit, information, and/or significance can I impart with brevity? Frankly, I have no idea.

So please indulge me while I run through some practice tweets:

@SusanSays, "#DemsLikedHillary'sLatestPantsSuit. Does anyone know if she had buccal implants?"

@SusanSays, "New poopie bags are inferior and have a tendency to tear. #DogPark. Be sure to bring hand wipes."

@SusanSays, "#Hashtag: this symbol would much prefer to be referred to by its other little-known but far more dignified name of 'octothorpe.' The name stems from cartography and means eight villages surrounding a field. This character is also used... (Uh-oh, ran out of characters.)

@SusanSays, "Check out the new Paul Newman postage stamp. #CelebrityPostageStamps. Bet you'll wish it wasn't self-stick!"

Hey, that wasn't so bad. And I only ran out of characters on one occasion. Sorry about that. I hope my tweets were helpful, informative, educational, and thought-provoking. And I just loved sharing.

I don't want to rush into anything, but as soon as I gain some more confidence, I believe I will consider expanding my social media presence. Instagram or Pinterest? Or perhaps sites like Tumblr and Flickr, and all the rest of Santa's reindeer. Can't wait to go viral!

So Where's the Duck?

W hy do I feel like I'm doomed to spend the rest of my days imprisoned in an old Groucho Marx quiz show, or a Monty Python movie? Not just any Monty Python movie, but specifically *Monty Python and the Holy Grail.* My captors do not permit me to romp through the entire film, but limit me to one scene, which, like in *Groundhog Day* (as long as we're using cinematic references), is repeated over and over again.

The scene I refer to is the one in which the knights, on the quest for the grail, arrive at a bridge which spans a dangerous ravine. Or maybe it's a river. (It's been a while.) They can either cross the bridge or plunge into whatever it is that's below. Their fate is in the hands of a twisted bridge-keeper who requires they each correctly answer three questions in order to gain safe passage.

When it's Sir Galahad's turn, he aces the first two questions, but unfortunately fails the third. He is asked, "What is your favorite color?" He answers, "Blue."

"Wrong," says the evil bridge keeper. And Galahad can go no further.

So what is it about the present that causes Groucho Marx and Monty Python to visit me on a daily basis? It's the dismaying sense that my existence is now controlled by a series of secret personal questions and a complex collection of letters and symbols which will gain me access to an entire universe of information and convenience. If only I could remember my password!

At first it was simple. When I started living life online, I created one clever password that I used for each new resource. That was all fine until I started having conversations with the Internet.

"No," it scolded me. "You can't do that. It isn't safe. Never use the same password twice. You need multiple passwords."

Okay. So I went about creating an additional clever password. But as it turned out, it was flawed. "No!" the Internet yelled at me again. "Your password is too weak. Try again." So now the Internet is judging me? This didn't seem right.

But the dialogue continued. "Your password isn't long enough. You need at least eight characters. Use a combination of upper and lowercase letters. Add some numbers. Throw in some symbols. No, don't use exclamation points or hash tags. They're so yesterday. Try an accent *aigu*." Accent aigu? My computer doesn't speak French.

As a result of all the advice and warnings, I am now the proud possessor of a long string of passwords whose construction reminds one of unpronounceable Eastern European names. Or they conjure up memories of Superman's archenemy, Mr. Mxyzptlk. But I have been informed by some unknown all-knowing source that my passwords, though unpronounceable, are safe. So what if I can no longer remember any of them?

Having to remember multiple cryptic passwords and your responses to secret personal questions does indeed put a great strain on the aging mind.

"It's time to change your password; you've had it long enough." What? No! It's a good password. You said it was safe. "But you can't keep it forever. That's not safe." I resist, but access is blocked to my account.

Because I was a dissident, I am now required to answer my personal secret question. *Who was your best friend in the 4th grade?* I type in a name. *Wrong!* And, like Sir Galahad, I can go no further. I am locked out until tomorrow, when I'm told I can try again. I had two best friends in the fourth grade. Is it fair that I'm being penalized because I was popular?

My various passwords are written down. Somewhere. But there are those times when iSusan and her iPad are away from home. In fact, it happened just the other day.

I was elsewhere and needed to access information from a particular website. I was asked for my password, which, of course, I could not remember. I tried several I thought might be correct, but none were. The little *forget password?* link seemed the only way out. I would change my password, then use the new password to access the site. I figured I could remember the new password for at least the time it would take me to enter it.

But wait. Before I was allowed to change the password, there was that message to deal with: *We want to make sure you are you.* And the secret question again, *Who was your best friend in the 4th grade?* I type in the name of my other best friend. Bingo! This time I nailed it. I was in.

Hey, Groucho. I finally got the secret word. So where's the duck?

Pecking Order

Recently, I've been giving a good deal of thought to kissing. In fact, I believe it's becoming a mild, and hopefully temporary, obsession. The type of kissing to which I'm referring is not the romantic, erotic "French" kiss (yes, I still remember those), but the less passionate and tongueless social kiss.

I'm fairly certain that the focus of all this wasted mental energy was triggered by our return to Florida one week ago. This brought about a series of reunions with friends and acquaintances whom we haven't seen in five or six months. The verbal greeting of, "Hi! How are you? You look great, considering what you've been through over the summer…" is inevitably followed by some version of lips-to-body-part contact. This is expected. But is it always desired?

How do I really know if the soon-to-be recipient of this somewhat invasive gesture really wants my magnanimous hello kiss, or are they worried that I haven't yet had my flu shot? If so, would a simple knuckle-bump suffice? Or, perhaps I don't feel like bestowing a kiss right now. Will he or she be insulted?

To paraphrase a quote from another famously obsessed individual: to kiss or not to kiss, that is the question. To move this soliloquy along, let's assume we agree to accept social kissing as a cultural norm. This solves one dilemma but raises a slew of other issues. For example, whom does one kiss?

I'm reminded of the Seinfeld episode called "The Hello Kiss" in which Kramer decides that everyone in their apartment building should stop living in loneliness and isolation and get to know each other. To this end, he has everyone post their name and photo on a wall in the lobby so they can all greet each other properly. Unfortunately for Jerry, the greetings from his new female "friends" are accompanied by a kiss on the cheek. Jerry recoils and announces to Kramer with great annoyance that "this kissing thing is over!"

The point for me is, is there a familiarity factor? How well should you know someone before it's okay to engage in lip-to-face contact? Should kissing be reserved for someone you've known for a while, or is a kiss anticipated even if I just met you last week? And if I saw you yesterday, and we meet again today, is it cool to skip the kiss ritual? Surely there must be rules.

Then there is the question of where to plant the kiss. There is the full-on-the-cheek kiss. The corner-of-the-mouth kiss. The closed-mouth, lip-to-lip kiss. Do both parties get a say in the matter? That's not practical. It happens way too quickly.

And, how many kisses are appropriate? Depending on your cultural preference, there are single kisses, double kisses, triple kisses, even quadruple kisses. When it comes to four, I'm inclined to agree with Seinfeld. This kissing thing might just be getting out of hand!

But if you follow the double or triple kiss protocol, where does one begin? Where do you plant the first kiss, right cheek or left? From what I've gleaned from the kissing literature, the right cheek should come first. Who knew?

What about mwah-mwah air kisses? Are they still considered disingenuous, reserved primarily for use by celebrities and *maître d's* in overpriced continental restaurants? Do they always come in twos? And if so, do they follow the multiple kiss rule of beginning with the right cheek?

Finally, there's the matter of hugging. Can hugging stand on its own as a kiss substitute, or does a mere hug not convey sufficient gladness on the occasion of the reunion? And if a hug accompanies a kiss, will that be regarded as entirely too intimate? What would Seinfeld say?

And what happens when we say goodbye? Must we deal with these decisions all over again?

While all these issues of appropriate human contact might be confusing, be glad you're not a canine. In the case of dogs, common greeting ritual involves walking circles around each other and engaging noses, not lips, as they sniff each other's butts.

Therefore, I'll take my chances with the social kiss. Even if I get it wrong.

Here's the Thing...

No doubt my priorities are all screwed up. There's so much going on in the world that cries out for serious attention and consideration, and here I sit, obsessing about Viagra commercials.

So maybe I'm concentrating on Viagra commercials because they're harmless, the only consequence of being affected by them being the possibility of a four-hour erection, and not a nuclear attack.

Oh, where is Bob Dole when you need him most? No, not to make a political comeback, but an ED comeback. He should be doing those Viagra commercials again and replace those horrid women who, with intimacy as genuine as a flea market version of a Gucci purse, discuss your husband's boner, or lack thereof.

Because when it came to erectile dysfunction, Bob Dole was the real deal. A survivor of prostate cancer, with genuine concerns about his performance both politically and in the bedroom, he didn't need to seductively gaze at his image in a mirror while running a brush through his brunette locks. His was an authentic first-person experience. He was forthright, dignified, and honest. It was a tale of ED that America could truly believe in.

What is it about the current Viagra commercials that make me want to vomit? Perhaps it's because I find all that oozing sensuality absolutely nauseating.

So here's the thing: if those commercials are talking to me so that I can convince "my man" to deal with his limp noodle, I would like to inform the ad agency here and now that I find it impossible to take serious advice, British accent notwithstanding, from women who look like they've been recruited from an escort service or an Internet porn site. Or if not an escort service, then perhaps 1-900-lez-do it. "Hey, big boy, just pop this little blue pill, and a good time is just a phone call away."

To say that these Viagra vignettes lack subtlety is like saying the Grand Canyon is just a hole in the ground: the tone of voice that is dripping with intimacy, the pouty mouth, the raised eyebrow, the sultry purr that says "you can trust me," the sly glance in the mirror, the hair released from those confining clips, the perfume applied to the wrist, then sniffed seductively.

Or, our temptress is lying on a bed or divan in a sensual pose, letting her locks cascade over her bare shoulders. And when she decides it's time to rise, she doesn't walk like a regular person, but slithers and slinks across the floor, glancing backward over her still bare milky white shoulder, with eyes that hold the promise of a hot night in the tree house. And the flower in her hair—an exotic touch. My compliments.

To the woman in the jersey, on the bed, fondling the football: I get it. But I just want to say that personally, I don't find watching football games all that exciting. In fact, I hate football. And cuddling in bed after? Well, fine, but who's going to scrape the left-over cheese dip from the nacho bowl from the pillow case?

And, by the way, when I want to curl up in bed with a good book, that's exactly what I want to do—curl up with a good book!

Also, I'm very suspect of the blonde in the blue dress floating around the room discussing the advantages of the Viagra single pack. Tell me she and that guy are not having an affair.

The thought has occurred to me that my criticism might be tinged with envy. Perhaps I would like the opportunity to be the voice of Viagra. It might take a couple of years, because I would have to let my hair grow. But that would give me time to figure out how to stretch out on my divan in a pose that best hides the belly fat.

But here's the thing: I don't think so. Being a middle-age know-it-all sex goddess is just not that appealing. Okay, so I'm no longer middle-age. Why quibble?

Now that I've aired this gripe, perhaps I can refocus my attention on global warming, and making sure my passport hasn't expired…and discovering the whereabouts of Bob Dole.

First published in July 2016

A Schticky Business

I admit I know next to nothing about current popular music.
When it comes to recognizing artists and songs, I dropped
out of those contests somewhere in the eighties. In fact, I have
a recurrent nightmare that I'm a contestant on the *Jeopardy!
Tournament of Champions,* and way ahead of my two challengers. Then comes the FINAL *Jeopardy!* category: Today's Top
Fifty, One-Name Artists. Luckily, I awaken just as I'm about
to write *Liberace.*

Although I have no clue about what is broadcasting
through the ear buds of some sixteen-year-old, I haven't failed
to notice a general escalation in music's weirdness. It appears
that it's no longer enough to have talent. In fact, talent may
not necessarily be required if you have a really good *schtick.*
(For those uninitiated in Yiddishisms, *schtick* is a German/
Yiddish word that literally means "piece," but in common
usage refers to a gimmick or someone's signature behavior.)

I'm desperately fighting the urge to say "in my day…" for
all of the obvious reasons, but I can't help but think of Frank

Sinatra, Ella Fitzgerald, and all of the other greats who just got up there and sang! But to be fair, we had our share of performers like the above-named Liberace, and Elvis, who were as famous for candelabras, gaudy outfits, and sequins, as for their talent.

The modern music business seems to be a breeding ground for *schtick*. I have only to think of some of the most popular divas over the recent years, like Cher, Madonna, and Cyndi Lauper, whose constant reinventions made you believe that every day could be Halloween. And Michael Jackson? Great performer, but also no shortage of gimmickry, white gloves and all.

Which brings me to today, to the one I had regarded as the current Reigning Queen of *Schtick*, the highly gifted musician and singer, Lady Gaga. That is, until a week ago, when I happened to watch *Saturday Night Live.*

I've been a fan of *SNL* since its inception in 1975, when staying awake past 11:30 PM on a Saturday night, or any other night, for that matter, was not the insurmountable challenge it is today. Currently, I might make it for five minutes of the opening skit, then it's lights out. But I digress.

For some unknown reason, on this particular Saturday night, I was wide awake. Okay, so maybe I was a little bit curious to watch Donald Trump, who was hosting, deliberately try to be funny. Or maybe it was the sausage pizza I had for dinner. I'm not sure. But one or the other was a sufficient stimulant. I was doing great. I rode along with the show right up to the musical guest segment, and heard Trump announce, "Ladies and gentlemen: Sia!"

What followed was the appearance of an apparition on the stage, which, judging from the shape of the body, I guessed was a woman. I say "guessed" because I never saw her face.

She was wearing a white, long, straight-haired wig with bangs that hung down past her nose. Where the bangs stopped, two cartoon-like Betty Boop eyes were painted on either side of where I figured her nose was located. This of course assumes that her face was actually constructed in a manner consistent with the human anatomy. (In light of her mysterious identity, I find it odd that she chooses to call herself "Sia." Is this her given name, or merely part of the *schtick?* "Hey," one wants to call out, "I can't see ya!" Haha!)

Oh, and let me not forget the giant black bow that sat on top of the wig, which, for some reason, conjured up images of Minnie Mouse. A short coatdress and very tall boots completed the outfit.

I have to admit I was both mesmerized and highly befuddled. Why would someone choose to look like she was just deposited on earth from a space ship? Was she a practitioner of some exotic religion that had not yet become mainstream? An escapee from Disney World? Or merely on her way to Comic-Con?

I believe she had a nice voice, but I couldn't really tell. She had a tendency to mumble in a Dylan-like fashion, but I could occasionally make out, "I'm alive; I'm still breathing," which was a giant relief since her bangs were covering her nose.

She was accompanied by another woman in a similar wig, but whose face was exposed. This poor woman appeared to be suffering, a conclusion I drew from watching her writhing, jerky movements, and the amount of time she spent on the floor. I thought someone should have immediately called 911. But in retrospect, I believe she was dancing.

I was intrigued. I forgot all about Donald, and did some checking into Sia. Where have I been? It seems that Sia (aka Sia Kate Isobelle Furler) is currently a very popular and prolific singer-songwriter hailing from Australia. She hides her face, she says, because she doesn't want to be recognized. She doesn't want to be famous. So she sang at the Grammy Awards, standing in a corner, body turned to the wall.

So, Sia—your persona is your "anti-fame manifesto?" Really? If you're so fame-phobic, why do you choose to perform before thousands of people? You can just keep writing songs for others to perform, while you yourself sing only in the shower, or along with your car radio, with the windows closed, like the rest of us. But, hey, what do I know? After all, here I am writing about you. And I highly doubt you're composing a song about me. So I guess *schtick* pays, and pays well.

And, like Liberace, Sia is no doubt "laughing all the way to the bank." That is, if she removes her wig long enough to find her way.

First published in November 2015

Getting in Touch with Your Inner Hostile Person

As an adult at the outermost limit of middle age, I admit to embracing two bits of pop psychology by which I try to live out my days: staying in touch with my inner child, and not sweating the small stuff.

Generally, these two popular wisdoms coexist side-by-side rather peaceably. In addition to being playful and potty-trained, I have also learned to be rather tranquil about life's little inconveniences. I try to keep my head when all around me are losing theirs, and I generally maintain a calm demeanor even while on hold for thirty minutes and being forced to listen to Kenny G.

If dates get canceled, they can be rescheduled. If I miss a train, there's always the next one. If I burn the toast, there's still another slice in the loaf. No need to get upset. That's me most of the time. Mature and dry.

Notice I said "most of the time." Hey, I don't claim to be perfect. Nor does my inner child. And like most children, she is prone to occasional temper tantrums.

There are definitely things in this life worse than Kenny G, things that deserve a good lashing from the dark side of my younger self. So I take an occasional holiday from tranquility and sublimely enjoy getting really ticked off! I'm not proud of the fact that I throw sponges at the television, but there are certain commercials that just drive me nuts. For instance, the two cardigan-clad women who claim that the biggest fright of their lives was losing their tooth enamel. And then there are those middle-age dames seductively prancing around in nightgowns, tossing their long locks, and making seductive eye-squints while a voice-over talks about vaginal dryness. I'd like to put them in a room with those dreamy couples from the Viagra and Cialis commercials and have them all deal with a four-hour erection.

But the juiciest TV tantrum of all is brought on by none other than toilet paper ads, especially the latest one that extols the virtue of ripples and its ability to let you drop your drawers. Oh please, lady, your refined British accent notwithstanding, are you really okay with the fact that you're getting paid to discuss shit? I can feel my temperature rising even as I write. So why, you might ask, don't I simply walk away, or mute the sound, or change the channel? Stop being sensible. I don't do any of these things because... I'm enjoying myself! Hey, my cranky inner child also deserves an outlet.

But yelling at the television is small potatoes when compared with the primary target of my latent temper—my local super-duper supermarket. The hostility rises within me even as I approach the parking lot, silently daring anyone to try to beat me out of a parking space. This response is triggered by the fact that I know before entering the store that they will be out of the exact items that brought me there in the first place. It happens all the time.

It's as if everyone in my town wants the same brand of cottage cheese on the same day, and I get there last! Or is it that the store is mismanaged and they can't seem to keep the shelves stocked? My money is on Option Number Two.

So I walk from aisle to aisle, getting grumpier by the minute. By the time I get to the checkout counter with whatever items I managed to salvage from my long list, I'm in quite a state. And, damn, I now have to get scanned by the smiliest, most pleasant checkout person in the entire store.

"Find everything okay?" she innocently asks in a voice so sweet it could send you into a diabetic coma. "No," I snap. "You were out of the cottage cheese again!" I don't stop there. I go on to describe the other items I couldn't find, how poorly managed I think the store is, and how I wouldn't be here at all if there was another supermarket within ten miles. She stares at me, clearly stunned, but somehow manages to stutter, "Have a nice day!"

My supermarket tantrum is not my dirty little secret. My husband is well aware of my Dr. Jekyll/Mr. Hyde dualism when it comes to stocking the larder. He hears me muttering under my breath as I make out my shopping list, and in the interest of not having me ram my car into a shopping cart, he has kindly offered to take on this domestic chore.

But no. I won't even consider it. Because, as in the case of those stupid television commercials, I derive some perverse pleasure from an occasional bout of foolish outrage. So I have granted my inner hostile person, young or old, the right to express her full emotional range. There's nothing quite as refreshing as a good hissy fit aimed at an inanimate object. (Apologies to the supermarket clerk.) Besides, perpetual tranquility can be such a bore.

'Tis the Season to Be Cranky

If it's Thanksgiving, can Christmas be far behind? Or does Christmas now start before Thanksgiving? Somehow I think it does.

At least a week before Turkey Day, or perhaps even more, as I innocently approached my local supermarket, I thought I heard the rather loud clanging of a bell. At first I thought it was someone's cell phone. "Poor guy," I thought, "He must be really hard of hearing to have his ring tone up so high." Or perhaps it was a fire drill? It was 85 degrees and I was in Florida. Can you blame me for not thinking about "Ho Ho Ho?"

But sure enough, there she was. The lady with the red stocking cap, sweat pouring from her brow, imploring us, in the spirit of the season, to deposit coins in her cauldron.

"The Season!" Why am I never quite prepared for this? Could it be because I exist in a subconscious state of denial about what will happen when my calendar flips from October to November? Surely I've been alive long enough to become wary sometime around Halloween. Or am I lulled into forgetfulness now that I live in the Sunshine State, where the closest thing to a snowflake is the white color of a golf ball?

The truth is I hate this time of year. And my irritability seems to increase in direct proportion to the number of candles on my birthday cake. An annual sense of dread overtakes me when I realize I can no longer escape the inescapable joy of the whole thing.

Regarding the commercialization of Christmas in this country, only the crassness of Las Vegas runs a close second. I shouldn't care. It's not even my holiday. But whether I claim it or not, it doesn't prevent my senses from being assaulted just about everywhere I turn. You might say it's sour grapes. And it's true that as a kid growing up Jewish in a Catholic neighborhood, I did suffer from crèche envy. But I've long gotten over that, as well as the fact that my childhood home had no chimney.

Rather, it's all that phony cheer and forced goodwill that gets to me, and the fact that I'm compelled to listen to recycled Christmas music in every store, every restaurant, every public place you can think of, including rest rooms. And if I have to watch *It's A Wonderful Life* one more time, I will personally push Jimmy Stuart off that bridge.

And the relentless, ridiculous TV commercials? When was the last time you received a Mercedes-Benz as a gift? And if you did, was it wrapped with the bow?

I detest that urgent call to buy, as if it was a violation of the Patriot Act to donate to a charity instead of purchasing useless gifts. Black Friday begins on Thursday. Cyber Monday begins on Saturday. My birthday is in February—will someone decide to move it to December? At this age, I can't afford to be rushed like that.

Each year I entertain a fantasy about running off to a place where no one has ever heard of Christmas, or Hanukkah, or Kwanzaa, and remaining there until at least December 31st just to play it safe. But I'm not sure such a place exists anymore, at least not where my frequent flyer miles will be honored.

So instead, I'm contemplating the construction of an underground shelter, or perhaps a safe room. I shall entomb myself there in early November, and you can pass me my Thanksgiving dinner through a slot in the door. I will consider emerging on New Year's Day, by which time my husband will have disposed of all the holiday cards, photos (except my grandchildren's), and heart-warming family year-end letters.

And all of this madness is supposed to be commemorating the birth of a key religious figure? You tell me, what would Jesus do?

And while you're thinking about that, did you know that there is reason to believe that Jesus, was not, in fact, actually born on December 25th? Don't take my word for it. Go ask Reverend Google. Legend has it that Jesus was born in the winter in Bethlehem, his birth heralded by a shepherd sitting on a hill tending his flock, who saw an unusually bright star in the sky. (Perhaps this was the first sighting of an alien space ship, and it actually took place in Roswell, New Mexico. Just sayin'.)

The reality is that a December night in Bethlehem is hardly conducive to hill-sitting, since it is cold and wet at that time of the year, and no shepherd worth his staff would plant his butt on the ground. Even the sheep were kept in shelters.

Instead, it is conjectured that Christmas as a birthday celebration is all wrong, and Jesus might actually have been born in warmer weather, say around August or early September.

But despite my intense seasonal displeasure, I dread the thought that this might be so. Because if it is, then heaven forbid, there goes Labor Day!

Let's Undo Lunch

I hate lunch. It is definitely my least favorite meal of the day. And by far the most boring. And also disruptive, much like an intermission during a play. Which I also hate. Not the play. The intermission. I frequently choose to skip it altogether. The lunch meal, not the play.

I have read that skipping meals isn't healthy. It sends your body's glucose levels plummeting, which in turn deprives the brain of energy. While I certainly don't want to deprive my brain of anything, it is, in fact, that very organ that has formed my attitude.

Remember Jiminy Cricket, the self-righteous insect with the top hat who was Pinocchio's conscience? I believe his cousin, Joey, has taken residence in my frontal lobe. I'm sure he's the one responsible for steering me past the temptations of the pizza parlor, the deli, and the pretentious little French bistro, and for me not pausing until he gets me to the salad bar. And I'm also working up a considerable hatred towards salads.

Except for lunch, I feel I have a reasonably healthy relationship with meals. Each morning, I consume a filling and nutritional breakfast, and look forward to dinner as a marker of the close of another day.

And think about it. How can you really enjoy a meal that is not consumed with an interesting beverage? In the morning, one can relish that life-infusing freshly brewed cup of coffee and at supper, a nice, relaxing glass of wine, or cocktail of your choice.

But what can you say about a meal that is usually accompanied by a glass of water? If you want to jazz it up a bit, you can get the kind with bubbles. They call it "sparkling" water, perhaps to convince you that it actually has some character.

Being a "retired" person, I no longer have a designated lunch hour built into my day. But for many years, I did. I would occasionally sit in a crowded coffee shop with a colleague and dare to eat a tuna fish sandwich.

But for the most part, I preferred to use that time for walking and window-shopping. Okay, so it wasn't always window-shopping. Sometimes it was actual shopping. *A lot of the time it was actual shopping.* It would have been far more economical to order that tuna fish sandwich, even if I didn't eat it.

Now that I write from home, I'm likely to wander to the kitchen, open the refrigerator, stare into it, and decide there's nothing to eat. Of course there's nothing to eat. I'm the one that does the grocery shopping and lunch food never makes it to the list. Perhaps there are leftovers from the previous evening, but somehow they seem less appealing in the light of a new day.

I realize that hating lunch has put me at a social disadvantage. As a rule, I don't tend to arrange lunch dates. Therefore, I don't get to see my friends as often as I might. If one of them should suggest meeting for lunch sometime, I might off-handedly agree. And the intent is sincere. I may even tell myself that this time it will be different. That I will actually follow up and arrange a date, for, let's say, 12:30 PM next Tuesday?

But the reality is quite different, and I pray that my friend, or by now, possibly former friend, is not sitting by the phone with her stomach growling. I hope all my friends have come to understand that I really do love them. It's lunch I hate.

There are those rare occasions when I actually do "do lunch." And I have to say the companionship is quite agreeable. If only it didn't involve eating lunch. I'm never the one to suggest a location. What difference would it make? Wherever we dine, Joey the Cricket automatically directs my eyes to the salad selection. With a glass of water on the side. No bubbles, please.

Perhaps one day in the not-too-distant-future (I'm at an age when it's best not to contemplate the distant future), I will be able to shed my concern about carbs and calories, and at 12:30 PM, enter the deli and order a big, fat sandwich on two pieces of fresh rye bread. Or duck in for a quick slice of pizza. Or indulge in a delicious triangle of quiche.

When that day finally arrives, and I grant myself permission to eat whatever the hell I really want, I just might possibly tell Joey to take a walk, and learn to love lunch. Or maybe Joey will just fade away. What's the life span of a cricket, anyway?

And Don't Call Me Elderly!

Thirty-seven years ago, before anyone would dare to refer to me as elderly, a movie was released called *Airplane*. Starring Leslie Nielsen, this spoof of Hollywood disaster films became an unlikely sensation. Of the many brilliant sight gags and clever lines, the brief dialogue between Nielsen and Robert Hays, containing the "Surely-Shirley" confusion, continues to bring a smile to my face.

Fortunately, over the intervening years, I have encountered only a few women named Shirley, which has limited the number of embarrassingly uncontrolled fits of giggling I've had. And, finally, I can borrow the line, or at least, paraphrase it, to air a grievance.

I'd like to deliver a message to the media, and I am serious. *Don't call me elderly!* In fact, don't call me anything at all. If you must state my age in your story, it should not require a modifier.

Whenever a news story appears about a seventy-three-year-old, for example, he or she is invariably referred to as "elderly." In fact, they are often labeled as "elderly" before you are even told their age. Here's an example: the headline states, "Elderly Woman Robs Bank." The story then goes on to report that Mamie Green, age sixty-nine, held up the Yucca City Bank at gun point, and eluded police by hiding in a tree. Now I ask you, should a sixty-nine-year-old woman who can wield a pistol, rob a bank, and climb a tree be called elderly?

Obviously this example is fictitious and a bit silly, and created to make a point. But there are very real examples. An NPR story reported on a seventy-one-year-old midwife and referred to her as "elderly." *Elderly!? Really?!!?* She's still working, delivering babies. There's nothing elderly about her these days, not even her age. And does labeling her as elderly enhance the story about midwifery? Totally irrelevant, if you ask me. If the woman was fifty-five, would NPR have referred to her as a "borderline middle-aged woman?"

If a woman of a certain age had the misfortune of getting hit by a bus, is that any more tragic than a forty-year-old being hit by a bus? Yet, you can be sure that the former would be cited as "Elderly Woman Gets Hit By a Bus," while the forty-year-old would merely be referred to as a "woman" who had the misfortune of crossing the street as the bus was pulling away from the curb. (In both cases, I'm happy to report the women survived.)

So what does "elderly" mean, exactly? The dictionary defines "elderly" as *past middle age and approaching the rest of life.* It then goes on to add parenthetically: *(sometimes considered offensive).*

The meaning of the word appears harmless enough. It's the connotation of the word that I find damaging. In our culture, the word "elderly" unfortunately carries the images of "frail," "feeble," and "dependent." And what robust seventy-five- or eighty-year-old wants to be lumped into that stereotype? I recognize that in some circles "elder" is not a four-letter word. If I was a member of a certain church, perhaps, or some Native American tribe, being called an elder would be an honor. I would be a respected advisor, a bestower of wisdom, perhaps even a goddess. I like the sound of that! (See "Romancing the Crone," page 82.)

But unfortunately, that is not the world in which most of us live. Instead, "elderly" is an ageist label. You might think that none of this is important, but words do shape attitudes and responses. So, what term should we use instead? Geezer? (Can a woman be a Geezer?) Long in the Tooth? Over the Hill? Mature? Senior Citizen? Or simply, Old? I don't have the answer, and as far as I can tell, neither does anyone else.

I like to think that age is more a matter of how you feel rather than the number of years you've been around. Therefore, I ask not to be assigned to a category based on the year in which I was born.

So, Leslie Nielsen, rest assured. Although you were the ripe old age of fifty-four when you made the career move from a romantic dramatic actor to comedy genius, I would never call you elderly.

ENDING ON A HIGH NOTE

What I Want To Be When I Grow Up (or, My Love Affair with Olivia Benson)

I consider myself to be a peaceable person. On a scale of 1 to 10, with 10 representing the highest tolerance for any situation that portends violence, I would rate myself a minus 5.

I'm against the death penalty. I bring a scarf to the movies so I can pull it over my eyes if the background music suggests that something ominous is pending.

I contribute to the ASPCA. I don't even kill the insects that find their way into my home, but instead, try to shoo them outside. Except for mosquitoes. But I consider that self-defense.

So I am at a complete loss to explain my fatal attraction to police dramas.

This is not a recent infatuation. It started when I was quite young, about the time I was first introduced to the phenomenon called *television!* One little friend was lucky enough to be the first kid on the block to own a TV. After school each day, five or six innocents would gather around the small box in his living room to watch cartoons, *The Small Fry Club*, and of course, *Howdy Doody*.

I clearly recall the afternoon of my transition from animation to criminal addiction. My aunt was visiting and I overheard her comment something to my mother which I thought related to my grandfather's health. My reaction quickly turned from grief to elation as soon as I realized that she, in fact, had not said that my beloved grandfather had gotten TB, but had bought a TV.

Now someone in my very own family had one! And thus began my almost daily visits to my grandparents to partake in the new American pastime.

Perhaps it's genetic, because one of the programs they regularly watched was called *Casey, Crime Photographer,* starring an actor named Darren McGavin. Each week, for thirty minutes, I watched Casey, camera and flashbulb always ready, solve crimes. I was smitten. Buffalo Bob Smith was *so* over, unless one afternoon he took an axe to Flub-A-Dub! (In actuality, "Casey" was so bad that it lasted only one season and I dare you to find a rerun, even on the most obscure cable station. But what did I know? Television was brand new and I was only ten.)

One evening, as we were watching Casey solving the murder of the week, I announced with conviction that that was what I wanted to do when I grew up. In response, my dear grandmother let out a shriek, which today I can only liken to Lenny Bruce's description of his disapproving aunt sounding like a Jewish sea gull, and gravely forbade me from even considering such a thing. It was much too dangerous. And besides, I was a girl.

I don't know if I consciously heeded her advice, but I never did become a detective. Instead, I became a speech therapist, and consoled myself with solving lisps instead of crimes. But my enthusiasm for car chases never waned.

If you are a fan of police procedurals, the following decades did not disappoint: *Dragnet (*"Just the facts, ma'am."*), The Thin Man, The Untouchables, FBI, Baretta, 77 Sunset Strip, Hawaii 50.* There were endearing tough guys, like Colombo in his smarmy trench coat (Wonder what he did on the weekends?), or Kojak on a perpetual sugar high from sucking his lollypop.

I love shows with the word "blue" in them: *Hill Street Blues, NYPD Blue,* and more recently, *Blue Bloods,* shows that rhyme: *Cold Case,* and *Without A Trace,* gritty shows: *The Wire,* highbrow PBS *Masterpiece Theatre* series with amazing British detectives, and finally, versions of *Sherlock Homes*, both old and new. And, hey Grandma, too bad you weren't around in the eighties to witness *Cagney and Lacey.*

What happened next was truly amazing. In 1990 the world was introduced to the first episode of the phenomenal *Law and Order*. Over the next nine years, I was a loyal fan. But in 1999 I realized that all those hours of watching were just foreplay compared to the climatic occurrence of the spin-off, *Law and Order: Special Victims Unit.*

I know I'm too old to have imaginary friends, but in my fantasy world Olivia Benson and Elliot Stabler are real people. I refer to them by their first names. I am enmeshed in their fictional existences, and Olivia's different hair styles. I've almost forgiven Elliot for retiring two years ago. The rest of the cast continues to change, but fifteen seasons later, thank goodness Olivia endures!

While all of the *Law and Order* series featured major roles for women, Olivia stands out. She is my hero. She is both strong and vulnerable, in a constant struggle to come to terms with her past. She is toughness with a soft core. She's fiercely dedicated to her job, loyal to her partner, and very smart.

She's fearless but cautious, charismatic but modest. She is empathetic towards the victims, and dedicated to bringing perpetrators to justice. She is everything that I would have wanted to be if I had not listened to my grandmother. Oh, and did I mention she is also a babe?

So please don't call me on Wednesday nights from 9:00 PM to 10:00 PM. For an hour, the outside world no longer exists for me as I escape into a new episode of *Law and Order: Special Victims Unit.* By the way, may I brag? Olivia has made captain.

SVU is the last of the *Law and Order* trilogy to remain with fresh shows each season. But we fans do not have to go hungry. There's a rerun on every minute of every day all over the dial. *L and O: Criminal Intent* officially ended in 2011, but Vincent D'Onofrio's tilted head can still be seen regularly if you are willing to flip through a hundred channels to find him. For his loyal followers, this is a small price to pay.

Perhaps being a pacifist and loving police dramas is not as incongruous as it may seem. In almost every episode, the bad guy is caught, wrongs are made right, justice prevails, and peace is restored. Isn't that a perfect world?

And speaking of perfect, want to know my idea of a perfect weekend? Rain in the forecast, and on TV, a *Law and Order* marathon. (CHUNG-CHUNG!)

There's a Hole in My Bucket List

I don't have a bucket list. There, I said it.

I hope this confession will not strip away my senior citizen discounts. After all, it has taken me years to get here and I deserve to ride for half-fare. But it had to be said. Even if I risk losing my benefits.

Having reached a certain age, I know I'm supposed to have one. In fact, just the other day a clever but meddlesome person suggested an item I might add to my bucket list, then looked at me with shock and disbelief when I told him that no such list existed. How could I possibly not have a catalog of unfulfilled goals that must be achieved before I expire?

Oh sure, you can have a bucket list at any age. However, when the days ahead of you are fewer than the days behind, the wisdom is that one must hasten to fulfill every last dream. Who needs that pressure at this time of their life?

The truth is, I can't imagine lying on my death bed, regretting that I had never gone zip lining. The truth is, I don't want to think about my death bed at all. Or about zip lining. The image of me hanging from a thin wire makes my shoulders hurt.

The very notion of a bucket list is depressing. The term derives from the phrase "kick the bucket," which derives from the act of ending one's life by placing a noose around the neck, standing on a pail, tossing the rope around a rafter, and when the rope is securely fastened, kicking the bucket out from under. Definitely more fatal than zip lining.

Since that 2007 movie with Jack Nicholson and Morgan Freeman, the imperative to create a bucket list is so great that there are actually numerous websites to help the unimaginative among us compile a collection of foolhardy feats, places to visit, and dumb things to eat that may or may not actually bring your final day closer to reality.

Seeking inspiration, I perused some of these sites and found them very helpful. I now have a separate list of 101 challenges I enthusiastically hope never to meet.

For example, I'm sure I can live happily for the rest of my life without the experience of sky diving. Much as I can live happily for the rest of my life without knowing what it feels like to get hit by a bus. I'm not afraid of heights, but slipping off the couch onto a rug is about as much free fall as I care to experience. Ditto for hang gliding, parasailing, and bungee jumping. I've already covered zip lining.

When I was younger, rock climbing and/or planting a flag on a high peak might have held some attraction. But at this point in life, the greatest physical challenge I care to accept is to once again be able to reach behind my back and fasten my bra.

I love sea life, but I'm not so crazy about water. So scratch cliff-jumping, swimming with sharks, scuba diving, and surfing. I have been whitewater rafting and managed to come away unscathed, save for a mild case of PTSD, so I think I'd rather not push it.

Despite the fact that it's land-based, Zorbing holds minimal appeal. Rolling down a hill inside a large plastic ball serves little purpose except to experience the adrenaline rush of a hamster.

I don't want to get a tattoo, although it might be interesting to adorn my body with more color variety than just brown spots. And nix the Brazilian wax. Call me modest, but I think I've passed the expiration date for undraping on a nude beach. And if I died tomorrow, I'm positive I'd have no regrets about never sampling chocolate-covered grasshoppers, learning a new language, being chased by bulls, or taking tuba lessons. Life has been good so far, and I've had the privilege of doing many things and visiting many places. It's not that I've been everywhere and seen everything. It's just that whatever I have left undone is far from mandatory.

But how's this for an idea of what to do with that empty bucket? How about filling it with fried chicken, and inviting some like-minded friends for a finger-lickin' meal? And don't forget the pie and ice cream for dessert. If I could do this just once without food-guilt, I'm sure I would die a happy woman!

Speaking of Sam...

Dear Readers,
        I beg your indulgence on two counts: one, for beginning this essay in the manner of an 18th century English novel, and two, for again writing about our new dog, Sam. I promise this will be the last time. Perhaps I shouldn't promise, but I will try my best not to further subject you to my excessive gushing over our fifteen-pound wonder. But today is Sam's birthday. He is one year old, and therefore deserving of another mention.

It's been two weeks, six days, twelve hours and forty-two minutes since we brought Sam home. And it's been years since we shared our home with a very young dog. Needless to say, there have been certain necessary adjustments to our household. Baby gates and other containment apparatuses are now part of the décor. My floors are strewn with rawhide chews that I have a tendency to step on with my bare feet. Thus, in addition to "sit," "stay," and "come," Sam has been learning many curse words.

And, then, of course, there are all the dog toys that squeak incessantly as he tries to rip out their guts. The other day a woman who I thought was my friend brought Sam a fuzzy duck toy that quacks nonstop as he squeezes it in his mouth. Unfortunately, it has become his favorite object. And I wonder what I did to cause her to hate me that much.

Getting used to a very small dog when one has been accustomed to cohabiting with very large dogs is another matter altogether. I had never stopped to consider that small dogs can be hazardous to your health. Unlike large dogs, they are below one's line of vision, so one must take special care not to step on them, or worse, trip over them. Clearly, I'm learning this the hard way.

Then there are those instances when I call Sam, once, twice, perhaps three times, only to look down at my feet and see him staring up at me in puzzlement. "Hey, I heard you the first time."

But it's been almost three weeks of delight, and lots of fun seeing the world through Sam's eyes. Although he was almost a year old when we brought him home, he behaved as if he was discovering everything for the very first time. Before us, he obviously led a very confined life. It's like he lived with the Mole Women, or was raised as Dog from *Room*.

During our walks along busy roads, I became aware that he was transfixed by moving cars and bicycles. And people. And other dogs. He backed away from path lights and irrigation flags. He barked challengingly at fire hydrants before realizing they were something he could conquer by lifting his leg.

Indoors also held many wonders. Since there are no second stories in underground shelters or utility sheds, Sam didn't quite know what to make of stairs. But when one's legs are only 6" long it is understandable that getting from one step to the next would seem as daunting as scaling the Empire State Building. But he figured it out, and now bounds up and down quite competently, looking very much like a Slinky.

Our stall shower is another object of complete fascination. He sits and stares at the water coming down as one might gawk at Niagara Falls. And he watches me intently as I step naked into it. I have to admit that I found it uncomfortable at first having a strange pair of male eyes gazing at my nakedness. That is, until I realized that unlike his human counterparts, Sam wouldn't be judging me. At least, I didn't think so.

He watches me blow dry my hair, Sam does. I can't begin to imagine how he might be interpreting this behavior. But at least he doesn't complain about the noise, unlike the other male I live with.

So all in all, the past two weeks, six days, twelve hours and forty-two minutes have been a delight. We haven't been sorry for a moment. Except perhaps for the incident when Sam ate a piece of baseboard molding in my husband's office.

His total cuteness impedes my efficiency because I have to stop what I'm doing to pick him up and cuddle; definitely one of the advantages of having a small dog. I now play second fiddle to a dog. I regularly listen to my spouse professing his love for Sam. But that's okay. Better Sam, than some bitch half my age.

But for all the joy that Sam brings us, we sometimes wonder if we jumped in too quickly, and didn't allow ourselves sufficient time to recover from the loss of Davis. But this quote I happened upon has been helpful: "Once you have had a wonderful dog, a life without one is diminished." So in another sense, having Sam is in commemoration of our other pets. The quote was attributed to the author Dean Koontz, and just goes to show that even writers of gory mysteries can have a soft spot when it comes to dogs.

So Happy Birthday Sam! May you live long and prosper! And may your energy keep the rest of us young.

Brisket Reconsidered

I'm so glad this holiday season is over. Because if I hear one more boast about brisket, I think I'm going to spray paint someone's Dutch oven. When did brisket emerge as the national dish of December? And where was I when this was happening? Clearly not in the supermarket purchasing Lipton's Onion Soup Mix.

I realized that I was living on the fringe of a cult when I innocently asked a few friends, "How was your holiday? Did your family join you?" The response was consistent—"Yes they did, and I made a brisket!" The pride factor was palpable.

Another aspect of this mania that I found utterly baffling was that each woman who rhapsodized about this fatty chunk of beef claimed to have the absolutely *best* brisket recipe ever, a family treasure handed down from Great-Aunt Selma, whose secret ingredient was whispered in the greatest confidence—"Grape jelly!" Or was it Coca-Cola? (Some weird stuff goes into brisket.)

And men were no better. Discussions about their floundering golf games were temporarily replaced by passionate praise of their wives' briskets. While it's flattering to be extolled by one's husband, I would prefer to be praised for, let's say, my looks, and/or my intelligence, and the fact that I am very adept at fixing paper jams in his printer.

Perhaps I couldn't share the culinary enthusiasm of my friends because my personal relationship with brisket did not have a good beginning. Let's just say that brisket and I got off on the wrong hoof.

My mother had many excellent qualities, but cooking wasn't one of them. Frequently, on Friday nights, or some other occasion that was supposed to be celebratory, she would set before the family a platter containing some gray-brown meat that reminded me of a cooked loafer. With ketchup. I told her I couldn't possibly eat this because it was ugly. She told me to go to my room. I reminded her that I didn't have a room. We lived in a small apartment.

But that was a long time ago, and childhood trauma notwithstanding, perhaps it was time to discover for myself what all the fuss was about. Since I had banished brisket from my life, I had never considered its source. In my mind, if my thoughts ever even turned in that direction, I had lumped it together with the rest of those fatty, ethnic cuts of beef that had to be cooked to death before it was edible. All of which, to my aesthetic sensibility, were equally as ugly.

So I decided to investigate. I began with one of those diagrams you sometimes see in meat markets, the one where the cow is divided into sections so it no longer looks a like an animal, but resembles a map of a small country. I find the drawing a bit disturbing, but educational. Upon completion of my research, this is what I learned:

Brisket (lower chest) is not flanken (short ribs) and flanken is not brisket. And neither of them, strictly speaking, are pot roast (chuck, upper chest). Roast beef is another matter altogether, coming from the end of the cow we would prefer not to think about.

Brisket is very talented. Brisket in brine turns into corned beef, while corned beef cured morphs into pastrami. And I have never regarded corned beef or pastrami as unappealing. So brisket is the ugly duckling, capable of becoming the Miss America of the kosher deli.

This may come as a shock to some, but Jews do not own brisket. In fact, it may be the most multicultural item on the planet. It is an inexpensive cut of beef, which lends itself to the culinary preferences of many different regions and nationalities.

The French cook it with bacon and cognac; Texans like it barbecued with Tex-Mex spices.

Each Eastern European country has its own version.

Asians love it. There are Thai briskets and Korean briskets. The Chinese like it with ginger, especially in restaurants on Sundays and Christmas.

Maybe there was something to all this passion. Perhaps brisket is the antidote for a bad day. If you're willing to put in the time, the result will be a succulent comfort food, right up there with meat loaf and mashed potatoes, replete with delicious gravy and a little horseradish sauce on the side.

I am now converted. New Year's resolution (just one): I will cook a brisket. Of course, mine will be the best recipe ever, giving my husband bragging rights at the next gathering of his friends.

And since it has such an international appeal, I say the next time world leaders sit down for a summit meeting, someone should serve a brisket. This formerly ugly meat could very well be our best hope for world peace!

Uncool Is the New Cool

I was at a gathering the other day when I overheard a remark that caused me to commit an impulsive act. I shot out of my chair, ran over to a perfect stranger, and delivered a huge bear hug.

This very large man, who could have been Tony Soprano's younger brother, was engaged in a conversation about popular music. His female companion, pointing a finger, had said in a mocking tone, "Don't ask his opinion. He likes Barry Manilow."

"You like Barry Manilow?" I repeated as I hugged him. "I love Barry Manilow. I have always loved Barry Manilow."

There! It was out in the open. Finally, after all this time. The relief was enormous, and completely overshadowed thirty-five years of derision, and the fact that we were now probably regarded as the two least-cool people in the room. Did I care?

Back in the seventies and eighties, rock ruled. You were supposed to like the Foo Fighters and Guns and Roses. If you were young, and a Barry Manilow fan, you kept it to yourself. That is, if you wanted to appear cool. Confessing that you liked his sincere ballads instead of angry lyrics condemned you to the purgatory of the terminally un-hip.

Among the uber-cool, Barry was regarded as a Las Vegas performer, a creator of songs to be played on elevators, and someone who sang to your mother. Does it get any worse than that?

But come on, people. It's time to own up. How many of you, like me, sang along to "Mandy" at the top of your lungs, in the privacy of your car? Or "Copa Cabana" in your shower?

And as long as we're on the subject, let me step out of the closet completely and confess to also liking ABBA (I dare you to resist dancing), The Carpenters (I chose one of theirs as my wedding song), and Kenny Rogers ("Lucille" was such a bitch!).

So who determines what's cool? Who's the decider? Not just in music, but in all things?

Is it the "Meh" list in *The New York Times Magazine?* Personally, I don't think that's cool at all. I think the list itself is the epitome of "Meh." And it certainly isn't cool that the print's so small! (For those of you not acquainted with "Meh," it's a lot like "Feh.")

Looking back over the years, you realize that what's cool is nothing more than a fad. Whether it was poodle skirts, James Dean, Mustang convertibles, or discos, every decade had its own coolness standards. A membership in the Playboy Club was once considered cool. (How lame was that?) Being a Playboy bunny? I'm not sure that was ever cool (well, maybe).

Gold chains on men were cool. So was Jennifer Aniston's haircut. How about wearing sunglasses indoors? Remember man-bags?

The list goes on. Icons of hip are forever changing.

I wonder, do we finally outgrow the need to be cool, or, as we age, does coolness switch gears from conformity to being your own person? I sincerely hope so, because I looked awful in a poodle skirt.

Besides, being cool is exhausting. I'm happy to skip right over all the information about what's "trending." Last year's hand bag will do just fine, and I'll wait until the hot new restaurant cools down before making it my scene. That is, if it lasts long enough.

I'm just happy that I know how to program the GPS in my car, and that I can text my grandkids. I think that's pretty cool!

And as for Barry Manilow? I recently read somewhere that he was #1 on a list of "10 Pop Artists for the Terminally Uncool," beating out the likes of Celine Dion and Cher. Way to go, Barry. As the song says, "Looks like we've made it!"

I'm proud to be uncool with you. I love you, Barry Manilow.

Fried White Potatoes

As much as I gripe about the tedium of the holiday season (see *'Tis The Season To Be Cranky*, page 135) I must confess that there is one time-honored December tradition to which I happily succumb. As soon as the calendar informs me that we are about to embark on the eight days of Hanukkah, I am overtaken by a compulsive urge to make *latkes*. Completely forgetting the horror of clean-up, I am motivated by visions of the succulent food with the delicious, crispy brown edges.

As an aside, one must always consult the calendar to verify the arrival of this holiday, because, unlike Christmas, it has no specific designated date. Rather, from year to year, it tends to hover over the month, and its descent is always a surprise. Not being a student of the Hebrew calendar, its landing always appeared to me as being completely arbitrary, although I'm sure that's not the case. But, like all Jewish holidays, it's never on time. It's either early or late. In fact, I can recall one year, in the not-so-distant past, when Hanukkah was so eager to arrive, it actually collided with Thanksgiving.

But back to *latkes.* For the uninitiated, a *latke* (pronounced *lat kuh,* with emphasis on the *lat*) may appear to be nothing more than a fried potato pancake. But in truth, the little *latke* is so much more. It's a fried potato pancake with a *soul.* The making and the eating is a treat for all the senses. Therefore, once a year, I say throw food caution to the wind, swallow an extra statin, and prepare to enjoy starch cooked in oil.

Actually, as a holiday tradition, it's all about the oil. Cooking with oil is a commemoration of the ravaged temple and the miracle of the small amount of olive oil that kept the eternal light burning for eight days, instead of just one. But it is not my intention here to retell the Hanukkah story. (If one is interested, one can always consult Rabbi Google.) Rather, it is to praise the *latke.*

Latke. I even love the sound of the word, which I find somewhat sensual. Uttered slowly and softly, letting the tip of the tongue rise to plant a gentle caress just behind the teeth, could there be a more loving term of endearment? *Come to me, my little latke.*

But like all things Jewish, the proper preparation of *latkes* is not without differences of opinion. Traditionalists claim that the only authentic way to make them is to grate the potatoes by hand. Since I don't believe that a preferred methodology is discussed in any biblical text, I stand with those who shred by food processor. The outcome is just as good, and one's knuckles remain intact. (Contrary to popular belief, knuckle blood is really not the secret ingredient in a good *latke.*)

I prefer to get my tactile fix from squeezing the liquid from the shredded potatoes, then combining the other ingredients with my ten digits. Want to release your inner child and relive the early developmental gratification of playing with your food?

There's nothing like being up to your elbows in potatoes, onions, eggs, and flour (or *matzoh* meal if you prefer).

And what can compare with the aroma of frying the *latke?* Nothing, except for eating the *latke.* Garnish as you like— apple sauce, sour cream, even caviar. And voilà! The dull potato has been elevated into a luxurious treat.

And I say fie on the spoilers who attempt to ruin the entire experience by suggesting healthy alternatives. Like baking, instead of frying. Or substituting other vegetables for the potato. A kale and cauliflower *latke?* Really?

And don't even think about using a prepared mix!

I confess there is a downside to this otherwise joyous experience. I must now begin to repair the damage that used to be my kitchen. But not even the splotches of potato starch that have landed on my floor and counters, or the splattered oil on my stove, can detract from my satisfaction.

And the secondary benefit? The memory of the experience that comes from the lingering odor of potatoes cooked in oil which will permeate the house long after the eight days have run their course. And once everything is nice and tidy, I know I will forget the mess and do it all over again next year. Whenever Hanukkah decides to arrive.

No "F" in the Way

As a "woman of a certain age" who attempts to chronicle life's nonsense with wit and wisdom, it is completely understandable that one of my role models should be Nora Ephron. To me, she was the gold standard. When it came to humorous essays from a female perspective, no one did it better. After all, what mature woman couldn't identify with feeling bad about her neck, or the belief that life would be better if only she could find the perfect handbag?

I will never be Nora, not even if I lived another hundred years and kept writing. But that's okay. I'm content to have her as the focus of my admiration and my muse. I evoke her name each time I sit down to write, and derive inspiration by asking myself, "Now what would Nora say?"

So when a friend happened to remark to me, "Your essays are so funny, you should really put them in a book," I immediately thought, "That's what Nora did."

Flattery notwithstanding, I could have let it go at that. But unfortunately, ideas often assume a life of their own.

And this one morphed into a disembodied voice, which might have been Nora's (or perhaps my mother's), that kept repeating, "So do it already!"

The idea of creating a book was daunting. Nevertheless, I decided to go for it. I spent the better part of last summer writing, rewriting, and organizing, and much to my own amazement, produced a cohesive manuscript consisting of fifty of my essays. Well, somewhat cohesive, anyway. After all, it was my first attempt.

But the 200-odd pages just sitting on my desk wasn't going to get me anywhere. Then, an acquaintance kindly offered to show it to an editor she knew at a publishing company. And so the journey began.

But the manuscript, professionally packaged according to the industry standards that I researched on Google, never got out of the box. The editor couldn't possibly read anything that wasn't submitted by an agent!

So my manuscript needed a middleman. Locating a literary agent was all that was standing between me and *The New York Times Best Seller* list. Surely this next step was not beyond the scope of my abilities. Wrong!

Looking on the Internet, which contained listings of thousands of agents, was not very fruitful, so I racked my brain to come up with anyone I knew who was a writer—and had an agent. Yes, there was that woman, the journalist, who had a few books to her credit. So with high hopes, I shot off an email. She politely replied that her agent represented only journalists whose last names started with letters from L to Z. If you fell into the A to K category, you had to look for someone else.

Yes, the literary world was highly specialized. It was necessary to define my genre. I did not write mysteries or science fiction, self-help books, or bodice-ripping romances. I wrote humorous personal essays. ("Like Nora," I wanted to scream to all those who ignored me.) The problem was, unless you were a famous person writing personal essays, no one was interested in what you had to say. Well, if no one was interested in what I had to say, how was I ever going to be a famous person? I seriously thought about changing my last name to Ephron. I didn't. Change my name, that is. But, so far, no agent, no editor, no publisher. Thus, like so many other frustrated new authors (notice I didn't say "young" authors), I decided to shortcut the journey and self-publish.

Self-publishing is a lot like regular publishing except that the exchange of money moves in a different direction. Instead of the publisher paying you for the right to print your book, you pay them for the right to print your book. And who knows? Perhaps my book would eventually sell enough copies so my heirs would each make $1.50.

And so the process began and nine months later, my baby was born. My book of essays, entitled *How Old Am I In Dog Years? And other thoughts about life from the far side of the hill* was a reality.

The book was officially released on May 12, 2015 with immediate distribution to Amazon, Barnes & Noble, and other online book sellers. There was a promise, but no guarantee, that the book would find its way into actual bookstores.

So you can imagine my surprise when I walked into my local Barnes & Noble book store, sauntered over to the humor section, and much to my sheer amazement and utter delight, realized there I was, on the shelf, spine following spine, nestled right up to Nora! I'm so glad that I didn't change my name. Because she's an "E" and I'm a "G." And there we will remain, side by side, me and my idol. As long as there's no "F" in the way!

Your Space or Mine?

Q uestion: what do a lion and a woman walking into her Zumba class have in common?

Before you make a phone call to the nearest mental health facility, please read further and allow me to explain my seemingly ridiculous question.

A fact about lions: they are very territorial and have been known to occupy the same area for generations. They are protective of their boundaries and will take on all challengers.

A fact about my friend walking into her Zumba class: she is very territorial about a certain spot on the dance floor that she has been occupying for years. When that spot was invaded, she, like the lion, engaged in confrontation with the challenger.

Amazed at herself for feeling so proprietary about a few square feet of wooden floor that really was, after all, public space, she felt compelled to share the story. Therefore, I became part of a small group of women, who, after listening, assured her that her behavior was perfectly understandable. Possession is, in fact, nine-tenths of the law, and each of us, under similar circumstances, would not have hesitated to bare our teeth and roar. She seemed comforted.

Was my friend's response to this invasion universal? I believe that it was. Like animals, humans exhibit territorial behavior that is definitely not limited to Zumba classes. There are so many examples in our everyday lives that I'm surprised we're not constantly engaged in turf wars.

Blame it on school. We start out with the very early social experience of having assigned seats in a group setting. Remember seating charts? Who we were and where we sat was represented by little cards which were placed in little slots. So we sat in the same seat every day to enable the teacher to remember our names. Do you see a pattern developing here? As a result of this programming, perhaps we develop a seating chart mentality which we carry into our adult lives.

Have you ever signed up for a lecture series that meets once a week? You choose a seat on the first night, and in doing so, unconsciously stake a claim. You might as well lift your leg and piss on it. It's yours. The second night, you return, and go directly to the same seat. So much easier than renegotiating the room each time. But on the third night, someone has taken your space.

Notice I said "your space" because you now think of it that way. Realistically, you know it's not yours. The seats are not reserved. Nevertheless, like my friend in the Zumba class, you are indignant. Responding to some primitive instinct, you want to confront this person and regain your stolen territory. You want to request, politely, or otherwise, that he get the hell out of your seat. But do you? Should you? I will leave that moral quandary in your hands.

There are many other examples: your favorite counter stool in the coffee shop, or bar stool at the bar, or table at a restaurant that you consider yours. We really do get attached to "place," even if it's outside of our private domain. And speaking of our private domain, personal space, while easier to control, continues to be something to which we feel entitled.

In your own home, don't you have what is known as "your" seat on the couch when you're watching TV? Or "your" chair at the dining table? And if your spouse or someone else should happen to occupy "your" spot, you have no qualms about reminding them that they were sitting in "your seat."

We are so familiar with this orientation that as guests for dinner at another's home, we are prone to ask, "Where would you like me to sit?" for fear of resting our tushes where someone else has already made an indelible indentation.

As for me, personally, while I do pride myself on my generous flexibility and highly evolved willingness to accommodate, there is a place where I am unrelenting. The left side of the bed is mine!

This is not open for discussion or negotiation. I invoke a higher power. It is my God-given right to sleep on the left side of the bed. In fact, I insisted this provision be included in my prenup. And this is not limited to my own bed. The same rule holds in a hotel, or when we are guests in someone's home. Even if we were camping out in a sleeping bag, which is most unlikely, the left side would still be mine.

Why the left side, you might ask? I really don't know. I have no logical explanation. But I do know that I would fiercely defend my thirty or so inches of the mattress. Perhaps it's only due to a long-term habit. Or maybe something deeper. It could be I'm just a romantic, but I like to think of it as the Law of the Jungle.

It's My Birthday and I'll Dye If I Want To

Like most women, I have a complicated relationship with birthdays. Which happens to be today. I won't get specific, but I will admit to being in my eighth decade, and creeping closer to the next round number. By the way, for those of you who, like me, almost failed math, the eighth decade does not mean I'm eighty—yet! Not that eighty is a bad place to be. It is definitely something I look forward to achieving—eventually.

While I am very grateful to be alive and feeling as well as I do, I can't reconcile the person who lives inside my head with the DOB that appears on my driver's license. I'm also very grateful to still have a driver's license.

Additionally, like most women, I also have a complicated relationship with my hair. (If you think comparing birthdays and hair is a non sequitur, please indulge me and keep reading. It is my birthday, after all.)

We believe that our hair represents us. It delivers a message to the world about how we see ourselves. Want to change the message? Change the hair. Are we in a bad mood?

Maybe we're having a bad hair day. Having a crisis? Go get highlights.

Over the years, I have tenderly nourished my hair with very expensive shampoos and conditioners, only to torture it five minutes later with a blow-dryer. I have alternately permed it, straightened it, let it grow long, and cut it really, really short. I've ironed it, taped it, and strangled it with rubber bands. And for more years than I care to remember, I saturated it with chemicals to hide the gray, which, of course, appeared prematurely.

But all that ended a while ago, on another significant birthday, when I decided to let my hair go *au naturale*. I didn't care if I was the only gray-haired lady in the room. My message was one of defiant confidence. And except for one brief encounter with the color purple, this is how I have remained. Until now.

My bravura continued until gray became the new blonde. Suddenly there were articles in fashion magazines and the *New York Times Styles* section reporting on countless glamorous, courageous women who were going gray! Even young people were putting gray streaks in their hair. I was no longer the lone woman in the room. I was part of a trend.

So, the other evening I was at a performance, and during intermission, I took my place in line to use the Ladies' Room. (Why are there never enough toilets?) To draw my attention away from my bladder, I began to study the group of women around me with similar needs. The head count was overwhelmingly gray. The trend had become a tsunami.

I exited the Ladies' Room feeling both relief and enlightenment. It was time for a new message.

Which brings us to today. This morning found me at the salon, bravely or stupidly, sitting in a chair for an hour and a half, while a colored streak was applied to my otherwise silver tresses. *It will eventually wash out*, I told myself. I could only hope the outcome would not compel me to wear a hat for the next six weeks.

I'm actually very pleased with the result. I think it provides a sense of fun. I'm not exactly sure what the message is, but maybe that's not the point. Hey, If you can't act out on your birthday, when can you?

In Defense of Dawdling

I'm here to state that, in my opinion, dawdling has gotten a bad rap. Look up the word in the dictionary (I used a few) and here's what you'll find: **Daw.dle:** *v, move slowly, take one's time, waste time, idle, linger, take more time than necessary, to spend time without haste or purpose.*

Does it not sound like a vice? Like a person who dares to dawdle is first cousin to a sloth? And isn't "sloth" one of the seven deadly sins? If this is so, then I am a sinner! Sew a big red "D" onto the front of my latest Michael Stars T-shirt because I am guilty of dawdling. And enjoying every depraved second of it!

Yes, I am an unabashed, unapologetic dawdler. I even like saying the word. To me, saying the word itself evokes its meaning. Try lingering on the first syllable with a gentle rounding of the lips and complete the second syllable only when you're good and ready. See what I mean?

It has been instilled in us from a young age that dawdling is morally undesirable. On a list of "Dos and Don'ts" for behaviors, dawdling definitely falls in the "Don't" column. "Don't dawdle over your breakfast. You'll be late for school." Or, "Stop dawdling, and go do your homework if you want to get into Harvard. So what if you're only in second grade." (In my case, I doubt it was dawdling that kept me out of Harvard. It was more likely my math scores.)

In life's second stage, we're the ones issuing the anti-dawdling warnings to our kids, as we rush to get them out the door in the morning, and perhaps ourselves off to work as well. After school, there are appointments, games, lessons, and rushing here and there with no time to spare.

And let's not forget shopping, preparing meals, doing laundry, and oh, yes, walking the family dog. And weekends bring little relief. No extra hour of sleep or a long, hot shower because our future A-Rod or Serena Williams has to be chauffeured to their games. After all, excelling in athletics looks really good on that Harvard application. Life at this stage is the antithesis of dawdling: it's perpetual motion.

Then the day finally comes when your last child leaves home for Punxsutawney State Junior College (you tried your best) and the color of life begins to change from fire-engine red to salmon. Not quite peaceful pink, because you still need to get yourself out the door each morning to arrive at work on time. And there's still the matter of the dog. Dawdling remains on hold.

Eventually you cross the magic threshold. You are a person of a certain age. You are a retired person of a certain age. Life finally takes on a pinkish glow. Not exactly my own personal favorite, but pink is associated with calm.

So Happy Birthday, folks, and congratulations! You have earned the right to dawdle.

As for me, I do my best dawdling at breakfast. I have never been a morning person, and frankly don't understand people who are. I've always relied on that first cup of coffee to get my engine going, whereas morning people act as if they had a caffeine drip inserted in their veins at bedtime. Getting myself and others out of the door each day was difficult, like slogging through peanut butter. Nevertheless, for all those years, I did what I had to do.

But now, mornings are luxurious. I actually look forward to getting out of bed. My life is finally in lockstep with my circadian rhythm, which doesn't awaken until about 10:00 AM. I'm usually up around 7:00 AM, and enthusiastically looking forward to taking my time. I manage to exchange a few grunts with my husband, who actually is much more of a morning person than I am, but chooses to remain horizontal until he smells the coffee.

I don't mind. I make my way down the stairs, followed by the dog who thankfully does not require any communication from me as I unlock the door and let him outside.

Soon the coffee is ready, breakfast is laid out, and my honey has padded to the kitchen with his newspapers. I slowly begin to sip the first cup. Aah! While leisurely sipping the second cup, I watch the news on TV. I reach for the crossword puzzle as a distraction from the latest depressing predicament. If I am successful, I reach for a second puzzle from the other newspaper. How much time has elapsed? An hour? More? The beauty is, it doesn't matter.

No early morning appointments, please. No breakfast dates, no golf games, no doctor's visits if at all possible. I am way too busy dawdling, and loving every precious second.

But, at some point do I spring into action or do I spend my entire day lingering over 1 Across and 9 Down? Actually, I don't. Linger, that is. There's that little cricket, Joey, who sits on my shoulder and warns me that my dawdling will turn into sloth if I spend one minute more in my bathrobe. It's time to get going, and that's fine.

I can be happily productive for the remaining hours, right up until bedtime. Because tomorrow morning brings a brand-new opportunity to once again do my very best to elevate dawdling to an art form. And maybe, just maybe, I will dawdle back to my computer to write. But first, another crossword.

About the Author

Susan Goldfein is the author of *How Old Am I in Dog Years? and other thoughts about life from the far side of the hill,* her first collection of essays, which earned her three awards for humor writing.

She turned to writing as a second career, following her retirement as Doctor Susan, speech pathologist, professor, and consultant. As a staunch advocate for reinvention at any age, she vows to continue chronicling the third act of life with wisdom and wit, as long as she can remember where she left her glasses.

Her essays have appeared in *The Palm Beach Post* and Hearst Publications. She writes a monthly humor column for the Florida-based newspaper *Lifestyles after 50*, and is a syndicated columnist with other publications aimed at the senior market. She is the author of the blog "Susan's Unfiltered Wit," *www.susansunfilteredwit.com.*

Hailing originally from New York, Susan currently lives in Florida with her husband, and their dog Sam, the world's cutest Russell Terrier.

THANK YOU FOR READING Susan Goldfein's *How to Complain When There's Nothing to Complain About: more thoughts about life from the far side of the hill.* If you enjoyed this book, kindly support the author by helping others find it. Here are some suggestions for your consideration:

- Write an online customer review
  wherever books are sold

- Gift this book to family and friends

- Share a photo of the book on social media and tag
  #SusanGoldfein and #HowToComplain

- Bring in Susan Goldfein as a speaker
  for your club or organization

- Suggest *How to Complain* to your local book club

- For bulk order inquiries, contact Citrine Publishing at
  (828) 585-7030 or Publisher@CitrinePublishing.com

- Meet Susan Goldfein and read her latest essays at
  www.SusansUnfilteredWit.com

48689410R00119

Made in the USA
Columbia, SC
13 January 2019